Children's
HUMAN BODY
Encyclopedia

Author: Steve Parker

Consultant: Dr Sue Mann

This edition produced by Tall Tree Ltd, London

This edition published by Parragon in 2008
Parragon
Queen Street House
4 Queen Street
Bath BA1 1HE, UK

ISBN 978-1-4075-1756-8

Printed in China

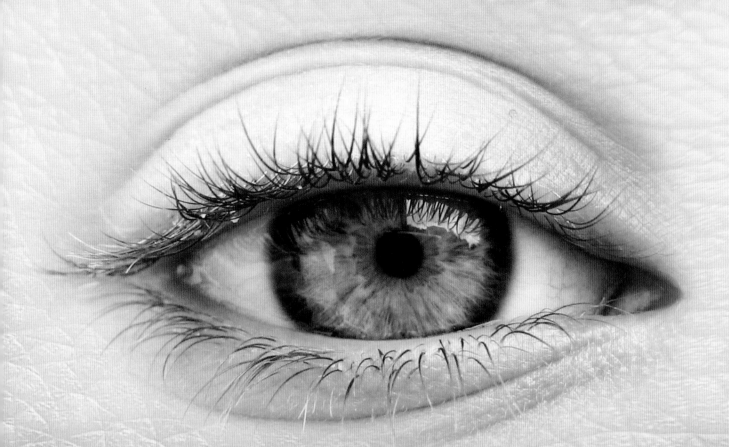

Children's
HUMAN BODY
Encyclopedia

Discover how our amazing bodies work

Steve Parker

Bath · New York · Singapore · Hong Kong · Cologne · Delhi · Melbourne

CONTENTS

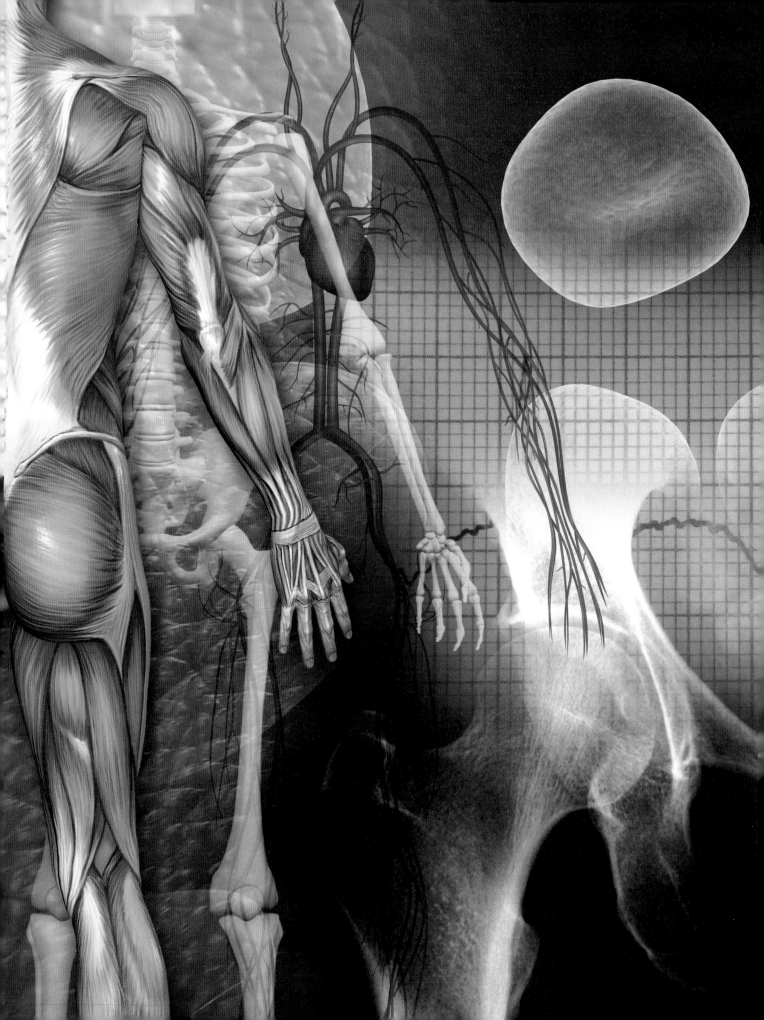

INTRODUCTION

As you settle down to rest, your body may seem quiet and relaxed, but under your skin, it is very busy. Different parts are hard at work – your heart beats to pump your blood, your lungs breathe to take in oxygen from the air, and your intestines break down your last meal. Millions of tiny cells multiply to replace worn-out parts, repair small everyday bumps and bruises, and make your whole body grow as you get older. Every now and then, your brain tells your muscles to pull on the bones of your skeleton, so that you can move about and get comfortable. If all this happens as you rest, imagine how active your body is when you are running at full speed!

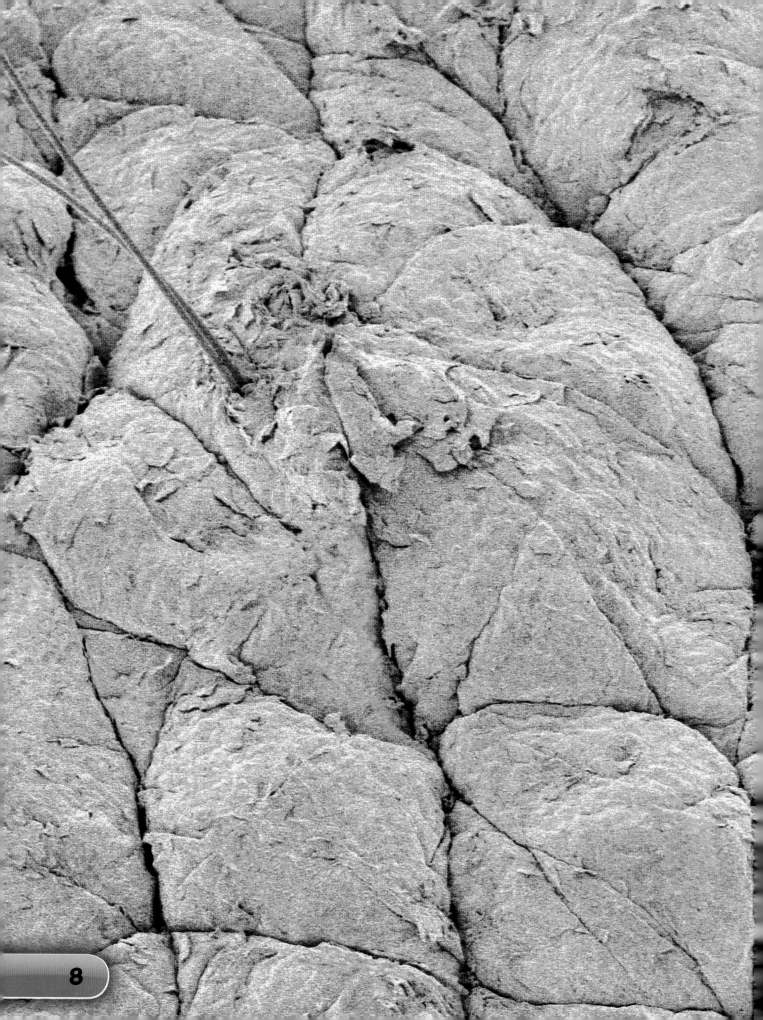

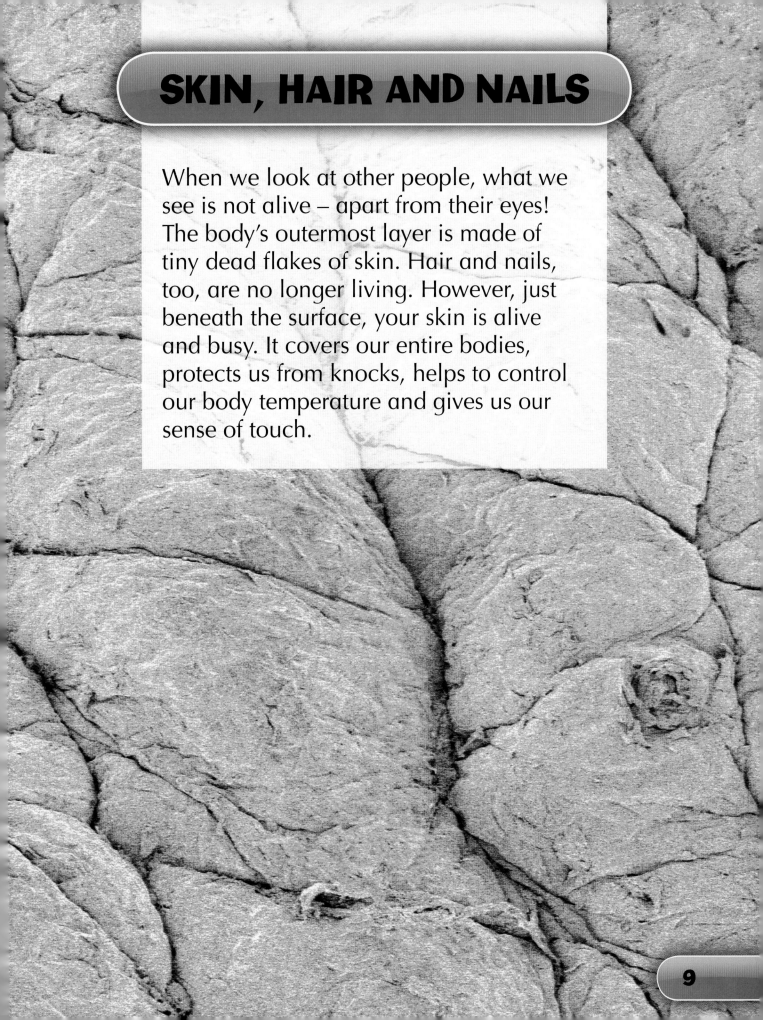

SKIN, HAIR AND NAILS

When we look at other people, what we see is not alive – apart from their eyes! The body's outermost layer is made of tiny dead flakes of skin. Hair and nails, too, are no longer living. However, just beneath the surface, your skin is alive and busy. It covers our entire bodies, protects us from knocks, helps to control our body temperature and gives us our sense of touch.

A closer look at skin

Your skin forms a tough barrier to keep out dirt, germs and harmful rays from the sun. It also stops your body from losing important fluids, salts and other substances. The skin, hair and nails together are known as the body's integumentary, or covering, system.

Skin's outer layer

Look through a microscope and you will see that skin has two layers. The outermost or upper layer is called the epidermis. This is made up mostly of dead skin cells and it provides the main protection. The epidermis varies in thickness on different parts of the body. Where there is more wear, such as on the soles of the feet, friction and rubbing cause the epidermis to grow thicker.

Fingerprints

The tips of your fingers have ridges of skin forming patterns of swirls, curls and loops, known as fingerprints. They help the skin to grip well. Every person has a unique pattern of fingerprints. A few animals, such as koalas, have fingerprints, too.

The inner layer

Beneath the epidermis is the lower layer of skin, which is called the dermis. The dermis is very flexible because it has tiny strands or fibres that allow it to stretch easily and then spring back into shape. The dermis also holds the roots of your skin's hairs (see right).

It's Amazing!

Every year, about 2 kilograms of your skin is rubbed off and flakes away. That's enough to fill a bucket!

A footballer sweats when he runs hard.

Cooling sweat

When your body gets hot, your skin releases sweat. This is called perspiration. The sweat flows out on to the skin's surface and draws heat from the body as it evaporates (turns into vapour). Even when cool, your body still makes small amounts of sweat, which is known as insensible perspiration.

Top Facts

- The total skin area of an average adult body would, if laid out flat, cover nearly 2 square metres.

- The weight of an adult's skin is around 3 kilograms.

- The thin skin on the eyelids is only 0.5 millimetres thick.

- The skin on the soles of the feet can measure more than 5 millimetres thick.

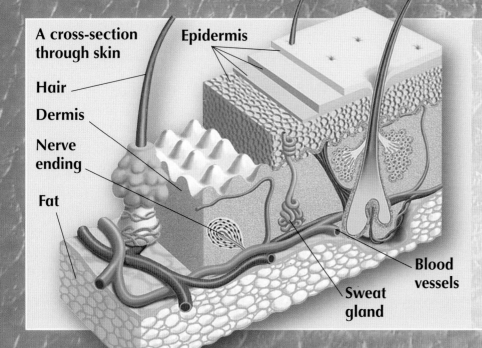

A cross-section through skin

Epidermis

Hair

Dermis

Nerve ending

Fat

Sweat gland

Blood vessels

Under the surface

The dermis layer of the skin is packed with millions of microscopic parts such as blood vessels (see pages 100–101), nerve endings for touch, pain and temperature (see page 17), and glands that make sweat. Just under the dermis is a layer of soft fat, which acts like a cushion to absorb bumps.

Always growing

Your skin may look the same from one day to the next but, all the time, tiny flakes are falling off or being rubbed away. This does not, however, leave you red and sore, as there are always more flakes forming to replace the lost ones.

A busy place

The epidermis constantly renews itself. Like all body parts, it is made of millions of microscopic 'building blocks' called cells. At the base of the epidermis these cells are very active. They continually split in two, to make more cells. These new cells gradually move towards the surface. They are pushed upwards as more and more new cells form beneath them.

A microscopic view of skin cells flaking off.

Skin cells in the epidermis

Stratum corneum

Stratum lucidum

Stratum granulosum

Stratum spinosum

Stratum basale

Melanocyte (see pages 14–15)

Epidermal layers

Cells multiply at the base of the epidermis, becoming flatter as they are pushed upwards. As they flatten, the cells die and become very hard. This flattening also produces a series of layers in the epidermis. From the bottom, these layers are the stratum *basale*, the stratum spinosum, the stratum granulosum, the stratum lucidum and the stratum corneum.

Up to one million dead skin cells fall off your skin every single minute. When you rub yourself dry after a shower or bath, even more wear away!

Chemicals and skin

Your skin is not entirely waterproof. Some chemicals, such as pesticides, can seep through skin into the tissues and blood, and spread around the body, causing harmful effects. Protective clothing, goggles and gloves help to keep these chemicals off the skin.

Wearing protective gloves is very important when handling chemicals.

Bubble of serum

Epidermis

Hair

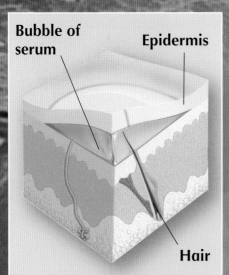

Cross-section of a blister

Up, up and away

As the epidermal cells move up, they change. They begin as box shapes and then slowly become flatter, like paving slabs. They also fill with a substance called keratin, which makes the skin cells tough and hard. Eventually, the cells become so full of keratin that they die. But they are still pushed upwards by more new cells below. After a journey lasting about four weeks, the flattened cells reach the surface. Here, they finally wear away as you move about, rub inside your clothes and press against things.

Friction blisters

A friction blister happens when the epidermis suffers sudden rubbing and wear. The top layers of the skin separate from the tissue beneath. Clear fluid, called serum, leaks from cells and blood vessels and collects to form a 'bubble' under the outer layer.

Rubbing your skin

- Spread out a clean, flat, black plastic sheet, such as a rubbish bag.
- Carefully rub your forearms or legs over the sheet. Not too hard – do not scratch or leave red marks.
- Look closely at the sheet. Can you see tiny pale specks? That's your skin. At least, it was!

Skin colour

People's skin colour varies, even within the same family. The basic colour of our skin is inherited from our parents, but it gets darker if we go out in the sun frequently. This is most noticeable in people who have pale skin to start with.

Melanin

Skin colour comes from tiny particles of pigment, a type of dark substance, called melanin. These particles are made by cells, melanocytes, which lie at the base of the epidermis. The melanocytes give their melanin to the surrounding skin cells. Strong sunlight makes the skin produce more melanin and go darker, which is known as a suntan.

Make sure your skin is protected by rubbing in sunscreen regularly.

Sunscreen

Protecting the skin against strong sunlight is very important, as it reduces the risk of skin cancer. Sunscreen lotions and creams filter out the harmful rays, especially UV-B (ultraviolet B). Such rays can pass through thin cloud, so you should rub in sunscreen protection, even on hazy summer days.

It's Amazing!

There are more than 10,000 melanocytes in an area of skin about the size of a fingernail. This number is much the same for everybody. In people with darker skin, the melanocytes are more active and make more melanin.

No colour

Very rarely, the skin produces little or no colouring substances. The result is an overall white or pale pink coloration of skin, hair and eyes, known as albinism. This can happen in animals, such as this peacock (right), and in humans, too.

An albino peacock

Sunburn

The higher amounts of melanin in a suntanned skin help to protect the skin and body parts beneath from the sun's rays. If strong sunlight shines on pale skin, it can cause painful sunburn, with redness and blisters forming in just an hour or two.

A group of children with different skin colours

Pigment cells

Melanocytes have long, finger-like extensions, called dendrites. These dendrites produce tiny particles of melanin. The melanin passes into surrounding cells, which then begin their journey to the surface (see page 12).

Epidermis

Melanocyte

Melanin grains

Melanocyte dendrites

Sense of touch

Your skin keeps you in touch with the world around you. You feel all kinds of sensations through your skin, from the gentle brush of a feather to a hard knock. But that's not all. What you think of as one sense – touch – is much more complicated than it seems.

Soft and smooth

The lips are very sensitive to touch, cold and warmth because they are packed with sensors. Babies often use their sensitive lips to investigate new objects, by picking the objects up and putting them in their mouths.

A varied sense

Even if you cannot see an object, you can find out a lot of information about it by touch. You can feel whether it is hard or soft, rough or smooth. You can find out its shape by feeling for edges, curves and flat parts. Your skin does all of this using millions of microscopic touch sensors that are mainly in the dermis.

Sensitive skin test

• Ask a friend to press gently on your skin with the blunt end of a pencil, using the same pressure each time.
• Look away while the friend tries your fingertips, palms, backs of your hands, and inside and outside of your wrists.
• Where is your skin most sensitive?

Braille uses a series of small, raised bumps on a page to represent letters and words. People with poor eyesight can 'read' these bumps, using the touch sensors in the fingers.

Part of body	Smallest distance for two points
Tongue	3 mm
Index finger	5 mm
Lips	7 mm
Palm of hand	18 mm
Forehead	18 mm
Back of hand	25 mm
Neck	30 mm
Back	40 mm

Two-point test

The two-point touch test finds the smallest distance between two points that can be felt by the skin on various body parts. The smaller the distance between the two points, the more sensitive the skin is in that area.

Micro-sensors

The microscopic sensors for touch are the blob-like ends of very thin nerve strands. There are several kinds of sensor, each with a different shape. Some are high up in the dermis, others are near its base (see pages 178–179). As the skin feels and presses, these sensors are stretched or squashed, and they send signals to the brain. The brain interprets the signals and recognizes what you are touching.

Merkel's endings   **Bulb of Krause**   **Pacinian ending**

It's Amazing!

Each of your fingertips has more than 10,000 microscopic sensors. This gives you a very delicate and precise sense of touch.

Nerve endings

Each type of nerve ending sends signals about different things. Merkel's endings send signals about delicate touches. Bulbs of Krause send signals about heavy pressure, vibration and very cold temperatures. Pacinian endings send signals about heavy pressure and fast vibration.

Temperature control

Humans, like cats, dogs and other mammals, are 'warm-blooded'. To work well and stay healthy, the human body needs to stay at a regular warm temperature of about 37 degrees Celsius. The skin plays a vital role in keeping this temperature steady.

Skin hairs stand on end to keep warm air next to the body.

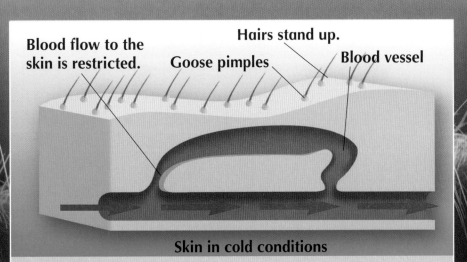

Blood flow to the skin is restricted.

Hairs stand up.

Goose pimples

Blood vessel

Skin in cold conditions

Saving heat

If the body becomes cold, the small blood vessels that lie near to the surface of the skin get narrower. This is called vasoconstriction. Less blood goes from the inside of the body to carry heat to the skin. This reduces loss of body warmth. Because less blood flows near the skin, it can make you look pale.

Getting too cold

In cold weather, the skin's tiny hairs have miniature muscles that pull them upright, forming 'goose pimples'. The upright hairs make a 'furry blanket', which helps to keep in body warmth. Your body's large muscles make small, fast movements to produce extra heat. This is called shivering.

It's Amazing!

The body has more than two million sweat glands. In very hot conditions they can produce almost a litre of sweat every hour. The water lost in sweat must be replaced by drinking a lot to avoid dehydration.

Keeping warm

At the end of strenuous exercise, such as running a marathon, the body is hot due to muscle activity. In cold conditions, a hot body can soon cool down too quickly. Shiny metal foil reflects heat and keeps in body warmth. It stops long-distance runners from getting too cold.

Runners wrapped in shiny blankets at the end of the New York Marathon.

Top Facts

- **If the body gets seriously hot, above 40°C, this is called hyperthermia or heatstroke.**

- **The body must be slowly cooled back to normal and rehydrated with plenty of drinks.**

- **If the body gets dangerously cold, below 35°C, this is called hypothermia or exposure.**

- **The body must be warmed gradually, preferably under medical supervision.**

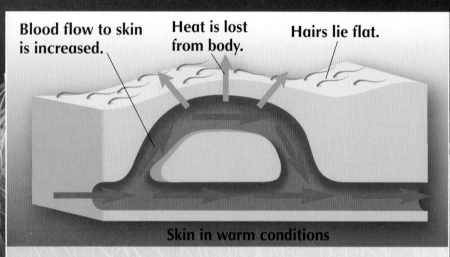

Blood flow to skin is increased.

Heat is lost from body.

Hairs lie flat.

Skin in warm conditions

Losing heat

When the body is hot, small blood vessels near the skin's surface widen. This is known as vasodilation. Vasodilation increases blood flow to the skin, which brings more heat from the body's interior. This increases the amount of heat that is lost to the air. As more blood flows to the skin, it can make you look flushed.

Getting too hot

In hot weather and when you exercise, your body heats up. Sweat glands produce watery sweat to help cool the body (see page 11). The tiny hairs on your skin also lie flat so that they do not stop air from flowing over your skin and taking away excess heat.

Cuts and wounds

The skin is your body's first defence against knocks and blows. Small cuts, scratches and bruises are common and the skin can repair these small wounds by itself. Bigger injuries may need help, such as stitches to close the wound and a bandage covering.

Sealing the wound

As soon as skin is injured, blood leaks from its tiny vessels. The vessels narrow to reduce the amount of blood loss. The damage also causes substances in the blood to form microscopic strands or fibres, called fibrin. These tangle together and trap platelets, which are small sticky cells found in blood (see pages 96–97). The fibres and platelets build up and trap red blood cells, forming a sticky lump called a clot. The clot stops more blood from leaking out and prevents dirt and germs from getting in.

An ice hockey player with a black (bruised) eye.

Bruises

A bruise is blood that leaks from damaged blood vessels under the skin. It can be red, blue or purple at first, but then changes to yellow as the blood slowly breaks down.

How skin heals

As a blood clot starts to form, white blood cells leak out of nearby blood vessels and enter the wound to deal with any possible infection (see pages 106–107). Once a hard scab has formed, dividing skin cells in the epidermis form a new layer of skin.

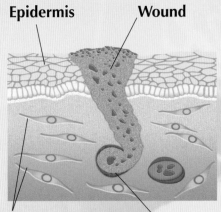

Epidermis   Wound

Dermis cells   Cut blood vessel

1. Damage caused to blood vessel

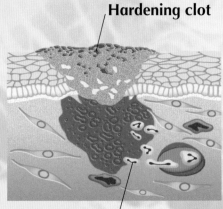

Hardening clot

White blood cell

2. Blood clot starts to harden

As good as new

Gradually, the clot hardens and dries into a tough covering known as a scab. Underneath, the skin's damaged edges begin to grow together, slowly forming new skin and closing the cut. Finally, the dry scab falls off, and the repair is complete. A big cut or wound may leave an area of skin that is slightly thicker and a different colour. This is called a scar.

Strands of fibrin (shown in yellow) trap red blood cells and platelets to form a clot.

Top Facts

- Some people are born lacking a substance in the blood that helps the blood to clot after an injury. If they cut themselves, the blood doesn't clot and keeps flowing. This condition is called haemophilia.

- In 1965, scientists discovered which clotting substances were missing. Today, haemophilia can be treated with injections of the missing substances.

It's Amazing!

When skin is mending a big cut, it produces a million extra microscopic cells every hour to heal the gap.

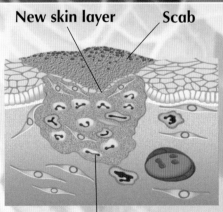

New skin layer   Scab

White blood cell

3. New skin layer forms

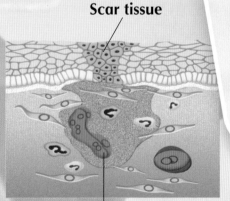

Scar tissue

Repaired blood vessel

4. Scar tissue forms

Hairy human

Who is hairier – a human being or a gorilla? Actually, they both have a similar number of hairs on their bodies. A human's body hairs are much shorter and thinner in most places, so we notice them less.

Scalp and body hair

The human body has different types of hairs on different parts. The main hairs are head or scalp hairs and these are thick and can grow very long if you do not cut them. There are also about five million tiny hairs over most of the body. These body hairs are usually small and soft, especially in babies and children. Only a few areas lack hair completely, such as the palms, the fingers and the soles of the feet.

A balding father and his long-haired daughter

It's Amazing!

The number of head hairs varies from one person to the next. People with light or fair hair have about 130,000 hairs. People with brown hair have about 110,000 hairs. People with black hair have about 100,000 hairs, and people with red or ginger hair have about 90,000 hairs.

Losing hair

There are different forms and causes of hair loss and baldness. In typical male-pattern hair loss, hair starts to thin on top of the head as the man gets older. The hairline at the front also recedes and joins the bald patch on top. This process is linked to the male hormone testosterone (see pages 210–211).

More types of hair

Your face has eyebrow and eyelash hairs. Eyebrows help to push aside sweat or rainwater, so it does not drip into the eyes. Eyelashes swish away tiny bits of floating dust as we blink, so they do not go into the eyes. Adult men and women also have underarm hair, and pubic hair between their legs.

An old man with a beard

Facial hair

Adult men have about 15,000 facial hairs, which can grow to form beards or moustaches. These hairs grow about 12.5 centimetres every year.

A male gorilla

How hairy is a gorilla?

Great apes, such as gorillas, have longer, coarser hairs over their bodies than humans, but they also have hair-free areas on their palms, fingers and soles, like we do. Gorillas have hairless areas on the face and chest, while these parts are much hairier in human males.

Brushing hair

- Using a new or completely clean hairbrush, brush your hair normally.
- How many hairs come out onto the brush?
- Do this several times through the day, and count the total number of hairs.
- Don't worry, in most people 50 to 100 hairs fall out naturally every day (see pages 24-25).

How hair grows

Hairs can look shiny and smooth or rough and crinkled, but they can never 'glow with life' – because they are dead! The only living part of a hair is its base, from where it grows and gets longer.

In the pits

A hair grows from a hair follicle. The hair lengthens as new microscopic cells add to its base or root. The cells quickly become hard and flat, like epidermis cells. The hair cells stick together to form a scaly-looking rod that slowly pushes upwards out of the follicle.

It's Amazing!

In most people, if the head hairs are not cut, they will grow to about 1.5 metres long before falling out naturally. But some people have unusual hair that can grow longer than 6 metres!

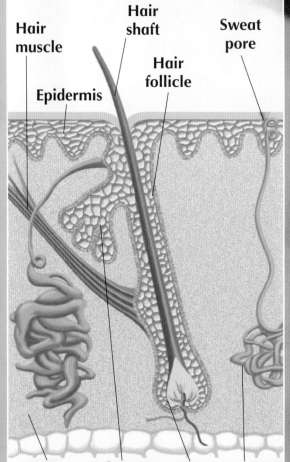

Hair muscle · Hair shaft · Sweat pore · Epidermis · Hair follicle

Dermis · Sebaceous gland · Hair root · Sweat gland

Hair follicle

The hair follicle is a fold in the epidermis that leads down into the dermis. The hair shaft grows up the follicle to the surface. The hair is linked to a muscle, which can pull the follicle so that the hair stands up (see page 18).

Hair shaft

Under a microscope, you can see the edges of the stuck-together flat cells on a hair shaft. Hair thickness varies from less than 0.05 mm to more than 0.1 mm across.

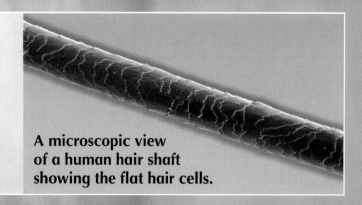

A microscopic view of a human hair shaft showing the flat hair cells.

Skin's natural oil

Next to each hair follicle is a tiny lump-like part called a sebaceous gland. This makes a slightly greasy substance, called sebum, which is skin's natural oil. It oozes up to the skin's surface and spreads out. Sebum keeps skin soft and supple. It also helps to repel water, and helps to kill germs.

A man with hair styled by cutting it and using chemicals to make it stand on end.

Natural hair

Hair can be straight, wavy, curly or frizzy. The natural style of your hair depends upon the cross-section of the thousands of hairs on your head, which can be almost circular or nearly flat.

A variety of natural hair styles

Top Facts

- Head hairs grow by about 3 millimetres each week.

- Fine, fair hair grows more slowly than thick, dark hair.

- After a hair falls out, the follicle 'rests' for up to six months.

- Then a new hair starts to grow from the same follicle.

Fingernails and toenails

Nails are very useful, not just for a quick scratch. They help to make the backs of the fingertips stiff, rather than floppy. This lets you judge the pressure of your grip more precisely, so you can pick up a delicate flower or a tiny pin.

How nails grow

Like hairs and the outer layer of skin, nails are made keratin (see page 13). The main sheet, or plate, of the nail is dead. It is only alive at its root, which is hidden under the skin of the finger or toe. As the nail lengthens from its root, it slides along the nail bed, towards the tip of the finger or toe.

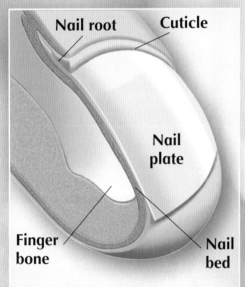

Nail root   Cuticle

Nail plate

Finger bone

Nail bed

Nail structure

The nail plate is a curved slab of keratin, which sits on the nail bed. Along its bottom edge is the sensitive skin of the nail lateral border, often called the cuticle or 'quick'.

It's Amazing!

Most people keep their nails neatly trimmed, to prevent snags and breaks. But some people let them grow and grow, until they reach more than 70 centimetres long!

The tip of the nail that overhangs the nail bed is called the free edge.

Faster and slower

Most nails grow about 12–14 millimetres each month. Fingernails grow slightly faster than toenails, and all nails grow faster in warm weather than in cold conditions. A knock or blow to the nail base can cause damage to the part of the nail forming there. This can create a ridge or lump, which grows along with the rest of the nail, until it can be cut away.

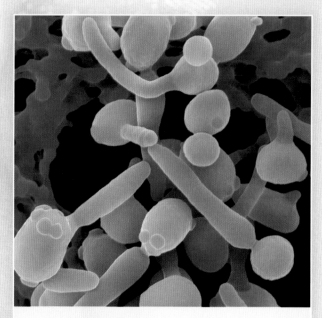

Nail fungus

Candida albicans (above) is a type of fungus that is fairly common on the human body. Sometimes, however, this fungus can grow out of control and cause infections. This can lead to painful inflammation around the nails, while the nails themselves can become ridged and brittle and change colour to green or yellow.

A lion's claws are usually pulled inside its paws so that they stay sharp.

Paws and claws

Keratin is also the substance that forms animal claws. Unlike your fingernails, a lion's claws are sharpened to a point so that they can tear through and grip any prey.

Nails and grip

- Before you trim your nails, carefully try to pick up a pin. It should be easy.
- Trim your nails neatly and wash your hands thoroughly.
- Try to pick up the pin again. Short nails, and dry skin without slightly sticky sebum oil, make it much harder.

Skin marks

Some people have natural marks or patches on their skin. These are normally harmless, but if a skin mark changes in some way, it's best to get expert medical advice.

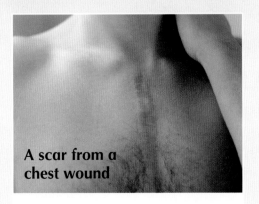

A scar from a chest wound

Scars

After surgery or an accident, the skin might not be able to heal itself fully. This can leave behind scar tissue (see page 21).

Naturally patchy

Moles are small, dark patches of skin. They usually start to appear at about the age of five or six. Moles that appear late in life or change their appearance (see page 31) should be checked by a doctor. An average person has between 10 and 40 moles of various sizes.

Moles

A mole is a patch of skin with more melanocytes (see page 15) than normal skin. This makes it darker than the skin around it. A mole on the face is sometimes called a beauty spot.

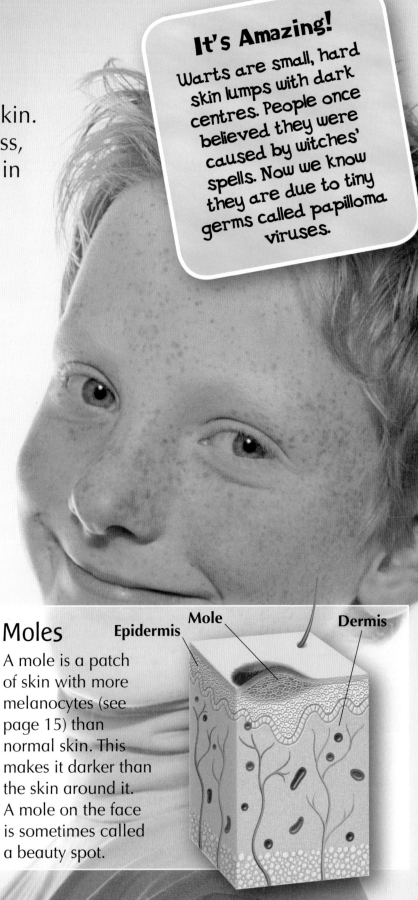

It's Amazing!

Warts are small, hard skin lumps with dark centres. People once believed they were caused by witches' spells. Now we know they are due to tiny germs called papilloma viruses.

Epidermis   Mole   Dermis

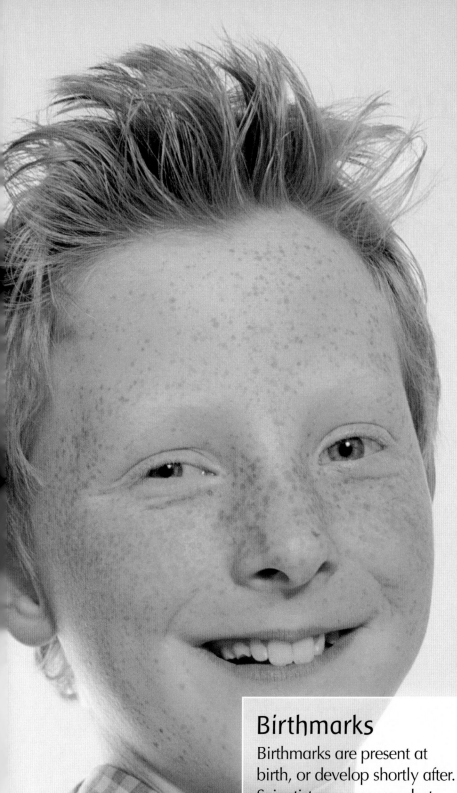

These fair-skinned twins have a lot of freckles on their faces.

Freckles

Freckles are small patches of skin that contain more of the natural pigment melanin (see page 15) than the surrounding areas. Freckles tend to occur on the face, shoulders and arms of people with light skin and fair, reddish or brown hair. They become more obvious when the skin is exposed to sunlight.

Birthmarks

Birthmarks are present at birth, or develop shortly after. Scientists are unsure what causes them, but there are many kinds, such as dark skin patches or strawberry birthmarks, which are lumpy, red patches.

A baby with a birthmark above her lips

Skin problems

Germs are always floating in the air and landing on our skin. If they get in through a cut or wound, they may cause an infection. Some skin infections – like boils – affect only a small area, while others cause larger marks and rashes on many body parts.

Spots and acne

Small spots called blackheads and whiteheads form when a skin pore or hair follicle gets blocked. The sebum (skin oil) made in the follicle cannot get out, so it builds up and may turn black. When you have more spots than usual, it is called acne. If germs get into a hair follicle, it swells and becomes a red and painful spot or boil.

Historical cures?

Long ago, people had many strange treatments for skin problems.

- Smear the skin with droppings (dung) from animals, such as cows or sheep.

- Put leeches (worm-like creatures) onto the skin to suck out the blood and 'poisons'.

- Tie a lump of fresh meat over the mark for a few days and then bury the meat in the earth.

It's Amazing!

Even on healthy skin, in an area the size of a fingernail, there may be more than 1000 bacteria. No wonder we are always being told to wash ourselves properly.

Blocked pores

Spots are formed when oily sebum builds up and clogs skin pores. Acne is facial spots that are common during the teenage years. This is due to a change in the natural body hormones in puberty (see pages 210–211). These hormones make the sebaceous glands more active.

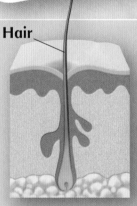

Hair **Blocked pore** **Pus**

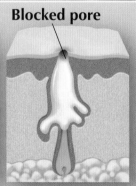
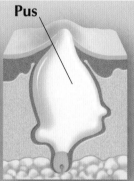

1. Each hair follicle is an opening for sebum.

2. The follicle opening, or pore, is blocked with dirt.

3. Sebum mixes with pus to form a yellow spot.

Eczema

Eczema is a skin condition where red, itchy patches form. These patches may be dry and scaly, or moist and weeping. The cause of eczema is not clear, but it is often linked with skin that is sensitive or allergic to certain substances, such as soaps, washing powders or cleaners. Some children with eczema have other allergic conditions, such as asthma or hay fever. Many children grow out of these conditions.

A small patch of eczema on a hand. Eczema can spread to cover large parts of the body.

Moles: changes to look for

A mole should be shown to a doctor if it changes in some way. The chart below lists some of the changes to look out for, which may mean the mole is harmful.

Normal mole

Normal moles may be concentrated in large numbers on the back, arms and chest.

Harmful moles

When one half of the mole does not match the other (not symmetrical).

When the edges of the mole are jagged and irregular.

When the colour of the mole varies.

When the diameter of the mole is larger than the width of a pencil.

Tattoos

A tattoo is a pattern of coloured inks put into the deeper levels of skin, usually by jabbing with some kind of needle. The inks are deep enough to remain for many years, and not grow out as the epidermal skin layer renews itself. Tattoos have been linked to skin cancer.

An automatic needle pushes ink under the skin's surface.

Skin, nail and hair care

Our skin has a rough, tough time. Bits of dirt, dust, germs, sweat and sebum (skin oil) smear onto it every minute of every day. If we don't clean our skin regularly, it becomes dirty and smelly and is at risk of infection and disease.

Good and bad

Skin is home to a lot of tiny organisms, such as bacteria. Some, such as *Proprionibacterium acnes*, are 'good'. They stop the growth of 'bad' bacteria. However, they can turn bad if they reach parts of the body where they shouldn't be, such as deep in a wound.

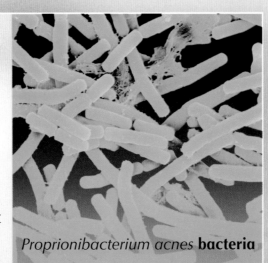

Proprionibacterium acnes **bacteria**

Keep it clean

We should wash our hands regularly, especially after using the toilet and before we handle food or eat, so we do not transfer germs to the food. Regular washing not only keeps skin clean and healthy, and lessens the risks of spots and rashes, it also helps to prevent other problems, such as food poisoning.

It's Amazing!

If your skin kept growing as usual but did not wear away at all, it would be as thick as an elephant's skin after just three years!

Keeping in trim

Whether head hair is short or long, it needs a regular wash and brush, and an occasional trim. Medicated shampoos help to reduce tiny pale flakes on the scalp, called dandruff. The more hair is coloured, dyed and heated, the weaker it becomes. Likewise, nails are less likely to snag, break or gather dirt underneath if they are trimmed short.

Washing hands helps to stop the spread of diseases.

Daily brush

Brushing or combing hair gets rid of tangles, dust, dirt and pests. Tangles and knots should be eased out from the hair ends, working towards the roots. Tugging hard at tangles makes them tighter and may damage the hairs or pull them out by their roots.

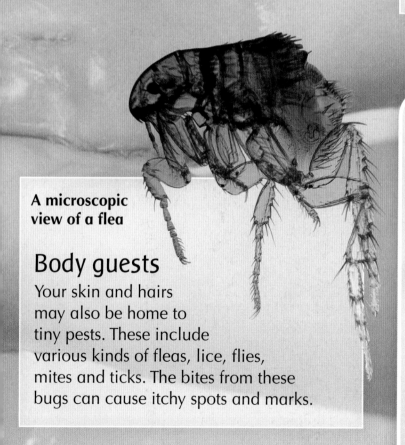

A microscopic view of a flea

Body guests

Your skin and hairs may also be home to tiny pests. These include various kinds of fleas, lice, flies, mites and ticks. The bites from these bugs can cause itchy spots and marks.

The best way to wash?

- After a day outside, using your hands a lot, you need to wash your hands clean.
- First, try rinsing them with just water. How much dirt comes off?
- Next, try using soap and water together. How much dirt comes off?
- Soap removes more dirt than just water because it sticks to dirt particles and pulls them away from your skin when it is rinsed away.

Bones, Joints and Muscles

Many parts of the body – such as the nerves, gut and blood vessels – are soft and floppy. But the whole body can stand up straight and strong because it has an inner, supporting framework of bones. Most bones are linked at moveable joints and are pulled by powerful muscles. Using bones, joints and muscles, we can make a wide range of movements, from writing our names to lifting heavy weights, and from leaping in the air to standing on tiptoes.

The Skeleton

All the bones together are called the skeletal system, or skeleton. Each bone is a certain size and shape, depending on its job. The arm and leg bones are long and tube shaped. The shoulder and hip bones are wide and flat to hold and anchor muscles (see pages 46–47).

Guarding the body

Some bones are protective. The dome of the skull bone at the top of the head protects the brain. The ribs in the chest are like the bars of a cage, guarding the soft lungs and pumping heart. The bowl-like shape of the hip bone protects the soft organs of the lower body.

These people are using their bones and muscles to push a car.

Ready, steady, push

As we push, muscles hold the skeleton and keep it in a strong position, allowing the bones to take the strain. The legs, back and arms transfer a forward force to the object being pushed.

Upper skull (*cranium*)

Lower jaw (*mandible*)

Neck bones (*cervical vertebrae*)

Collarbone (*clavicle*)

Shoulder blade (*scapula*)

Breastbone (*sternum*)

Upper arm bone (*humerus*)

Hip bone (*pelvis*)

Ribs

Forearm bones (*ulna, radius*)

Finger bones (*phalanges*)

Lower backbones (*lumbar vertebrae*)

Not too stiff

Bones are hard, but they are not completely rigid, or stiff, especially in children and young people. This means they can bend slightly to take great strain rather than cracking or snapping. Bones are light yet tough – weight for weight, they are stronger than most metals and high-tech plastics. And bones can do what metals and plastics cannot – if they are damaged, they can mend themselves.

The main bones of the human skeleton with their scientific names

Thigh bone (*femur*)

Kneecap (*patella*)

Lower leg bones (*fibula, tibia*)

Foot bones (*tarsals*)

Toe bones (*phalanges*)

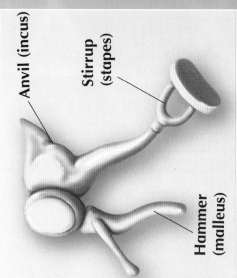

Anvil (incus)

Stirrup (stapes)

Hammer (malleus)

Smallest bones

The smallest bones are the hammer, anvil and stirrup inside the ear. Each of these tiny bones is about 0.5 centimetres long. They are known as the auditory ossicles and they carry sound from the eardrum to the innermost part of the ear, the cochlea (see pages 172–173).

It's Amazing!

The longest bone is the femur, or thigh bone, which forms one quarter of the body's height. The shortest bone is the stirrup in the ear.

Robert Wadlow in 1938

Outsized skeleton

The height of the body depends on the size of the skeleton. The tallest person ever, at 2.73 metres, was Robert Wadlow (1918–1940) of the USA. His thigh bone alone was half the height of a normal adult.

Inside a bone

A typical bone is not solid. The strongest part is the outer layer called compact bone. Inside this is a layer known as cancellous bone, with holes like a sponge. And inside this, in the middle of the bone, is a soft, jelly-like substance called bone marrow.

Lamella

Magnified view of haversian systems in compact bone

Haversian systems

Compact bone is made of thousands of tiny rod-like parts called haversian systems. At the middle of each of these is a hole carrying blood vessels and nerves. Each hole is surrounded by circular layers of bone, called lamellae.

Fibres and minerals

Bone tissue contains a network of tiny fibres made of a substance called collagen. It also contains hard crystals of the minerals calcium carbonate and calcium phosphate. These crystals are scattered among the collagen fibres. The fibres are flexible and allow the bones to bend slightly, while the minerals make the bones very hard.

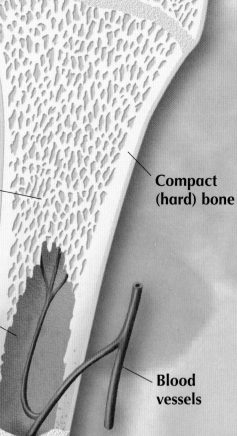

Cancellous (spongy) bone

Medullary cavity containing bone marrow

Compact (hard) bone

Blood vessels

Cutaway view of a typical long bone showing compact bone, cancellous bone and bone marrow.

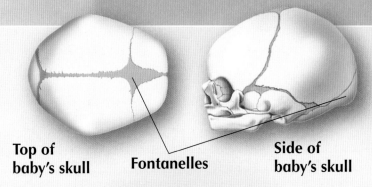

Top of
baby's skull

Fontanelles

Side of
baby's skull

Holes in the head

A newborn baby's skull has slight gaps, called
fontanelles, between some of its skull bones.
These soft areas are squashed together during
birth to help the baby's passage through the
cervix (see pages 200–201).

Inside the bone

The strands that make up the spongy bone are
arranged so that they can absorb the stresses
and strains that we put on them as we go
through our daily lives. In our longest bones,
such as those in our legs, the spongy bone gives
way to the medullary cavity, an opening that
is full of bone marrow (see below).

Red blood cell

White blood cell

**Magnified view of blood cells
in bone marrow**

Blood cells

The bone marrow makes
new blood cells (see
pages 96–97) to replace
old cells that die. The
blood cells all start out
the same but then change
as they develop to form
red blood cells, white
blood cells and platelets.

Top Facts

- A human skeleton
  made of steel would
  weigh five times
  more than a real
  skeleton of bones.

- If bones have to
  cope regularly with
  doing more work –
  for example, by
  lifting weights –
  they grow thicker
  and stronger.

- When we get older,
  we lose some of the
  minerals that make
  up our bones. This
  can make them
  brittle and they can
  break more easily
  than when we are
  younger.

It's Amazing!

There are about
2.4 kilograms of
marrow in an adult's
bones. The bone marrow
produces more than
three million new blood
cells every second.

Skull and spine

The main bone inside the head is the skull. The bones at the front of the skull form the face. Below the skull is the spine, which runs down through the neck, chest and lower back to the hips.

Head bones

The dome-shaped part of the skull around the brain is called the cranium, and it is made of eight curved bones. Nearly all of the skull bones are joined together, most of them by immovable joints (see page 43). Only one of the bones can move – the mandible, or lower jaw, which forms the chin. It moves at the joints just below each ear.

A mountain biker wears a helmet to protect her head. People who take part in dangerous sports may need to wear extra protection.

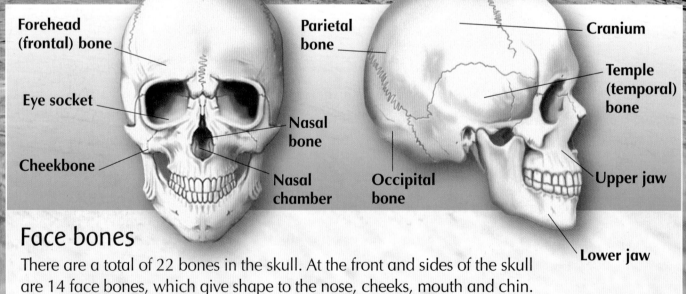

Forehead (frontal) bone

Eye socket

Cheekbone

Parietal bone

Nasal bone

Nasal chamber

Occipital bone

Cranium

Temple (temporal) bone

Upper jaw

Lower jaw

Face bones

There are a total of 22 bones in the skull. At the front and sides of the skull are 14 face bones, which give shape to the nose, cheeks, mouth and chin.

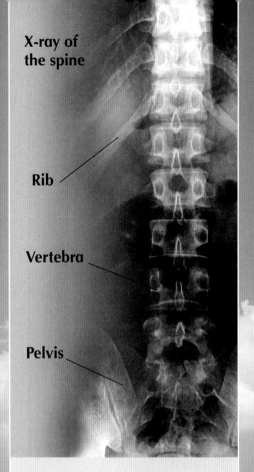

X-ray of
the spine

Rib

Vertebra

Pelvis

Tower of bones

The spine is made up of a 'tower' of tube-like bones, called vertebrae (as shown in the X-ray above). Each vertebra is separated from its neighbours by a slightly squashy disc.

Curved and tube bones

- Try to bend a flat piece of thin card. It's easy to do.
- Roll the card into a tube shape and fix it with some sticky tape.
- Try to bend the tube. It's much harder to do.
- Many bones are curved, like the skull bones, or tube shaped, like vertebrae, because it makes them much stronger than if they were flat.

Main support

The spine, or backbone, is the body's main central support. It is made up of 24 vertebrae (see left), with 7 in the neck, 12 in the chest and 5 in the lower back. Below this are two sets of fused bones called the sacrum and the coccyx. Each vertebra can move only slightly against the one next to it, but over the whole backbone, these small movements allow the back to bend a long way.

A paralyzed woman using a wheelchair because she cannot move her legs.

It's Amazing!

Did you know that the human body has a 'tail'? The coccyx is a very short, stubby bone at the base of the backbone. Luckily, we cannot see it on the outside.

Spinal injury

Running up the middle of the vertebrae is the spinal cord (see pages 150–151), which is the body's main nerve. Damage to the spinal column can stop the spinal cord carrying messages around the body, which can lead to paralysis, or the inability to move certain limbs.

Joining bones

Your bones would fall apart if they were not fastened together by joints. Each joint lets your bones move in a certain direction and by a particular amount. All together, the joints allow your body to move into an amazing variety of positions.

On the move

Joints are classified by two methods: their structure and the movement they produce. A joint's structure depends upon many different things. These include whether the joint is stuck tightly together to form a suture (see page 43), or whether it contains cartilage to make the bone movement easier (see page 44).

Types of joints

In some joints, the ball-shaped end of one bone fits into a bowl-shaped socket in the other bone. These ball-and-socket joints let the bones move to and fro and sideways and allow them to twist. They are found in the shoulder and hip. In hinge joints, the bones can move to and fro but not sideways. Hinge joints are found in the knees and the finger knuckles.

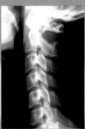
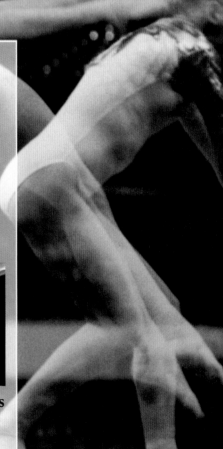
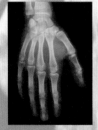

| Gliding joints in the hand | Ball-and-socket joint in the hip | Hinge joint in the knee | Many joints in the spine |

Lots of joints

Some joints have more than two bones – for example, there are eight bones in the wrist and seven in the ankle. Each of these bones links to those next to it via a gliding joint, in which the bones slide and tilt against each other. The joints in the wrist are flexible, and they allow the hand to move in many positions. The joints in the ankle are less bendy but much stronger so that they can support the weight of the body.

This gymnast's joints allow her body to move into many different positions.

It's Amazing!
The body's tiniest joint is on the smallest bone, the stirrup, deep inside the ear. The whole joint is smaller than this letter 'o'.

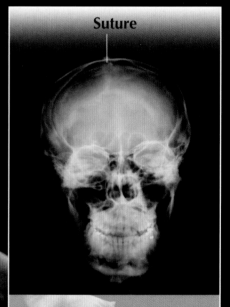

Suture

Ready to throw

Throwing a ball is good example of how the joints all work together. Just before the ball is released, the joints of the hips, back, shoulder, elbow, wrist and fingers all move in a fast sequence, one after the other, to hurl the ball at great speed.

A baseball pitcher 'winds up' before releasing the ball.

Skull joints

An adult's skull bones are joined together with strong fibres set into a kind of glue. These fixed, or immovable, joints look like wiggly lines and are known as sutures.

Inside a joint

Although the joints allow us to get about, their movement has to be restricted, otherwise the bones could move too far and damage themselves. The joints also have to be well lubricated to keep the bones sliding smoothly and to stop them from wearing away.

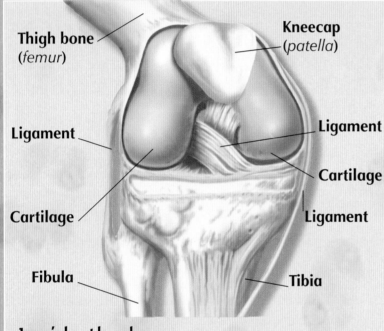

Thigh bone (femur)

Kneecap (patella)

Ligament

Ligament

Cartilage

Cartilage

Ligament

Fibula

Tibia

Inside the knee

The knee joint connects the bones of the upper and lower leg. The bones are connected by strong cord-like tissues called ligaments (see right). Protecting the knee joint is a small bony cap, called the patella, or kneecap.

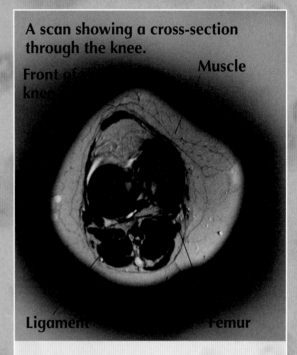

A scan showing a cross-section through the knee.

Front of knee

Muscle

Ligament

Femur

Knee scan

This MRI scan (see pages 160–161), shows inside the knee joint, including the ligaments, muscle tissue and bones.

Cartilage cushion

Inside a joint, the ends of the bones are covered by a substance called cartilage, which is springy and smooth and protects the bone ends. It forms a tough cushion so that the bones do not crack or splinter when the joint is knocked. The synovial capsule that surrounds the joint makes a slippery liquid called synovial fluid. This works like oil in an engine – it stops the bones from scraping and keeps the joint working smoothly.

A magnified
image of cartilage

Artificial joints

- Sometimes, a joint becomes too stiff and painful. To relieve the pain, the joint can be replaced with an artificial one.

- One of the most common artificial joints is the hip.

- The first artificial hip operations were carried out in the 1960s by English surgeon John Charnley.

- Today, about 1 person in 30 over the age of 55 years old has an artificial hip. Some people even have two of them.

Safety straps

The ligaments are long, stretchy straps that run across joints and attach bones to each other. They work like safety belts in a car by holding the joints together in their correct place and stopping them from falling apart.

Arthritic hand

In a disease called osteoarthritis, the cartilage covering the bones in the joints becomes cracked and flaky. The synovial capsules thicken and the bones grow lumps and bumps. These make the joints swell up, and this makes any movement difficult and painful. In this X-ray of a hand holding a pen (right), the joints are swollen and the bones are misshapen, indicating that this person has severe osteoarthritis.

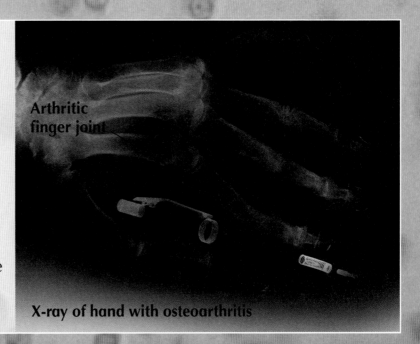

Arthritic
finger joint

X-ray of hand with osteoarthritis

Muscles

Almost half of the body is made of muscles. There are hundreds of them, and they power every movement we make. Muscles are actually designed to carry out just one task – get shorter.

Skeletal muscles

Most of the body's muscles are skeletal muscles. These muscles are involved in moving our head, neck, limbs and torso. They are attached to the bones of the skeleton by tough, rope-like tendons, as opposed to the ligaments that attach the bones to each other. For example, the Achilles tendon attaches the calf muscle to the heel.

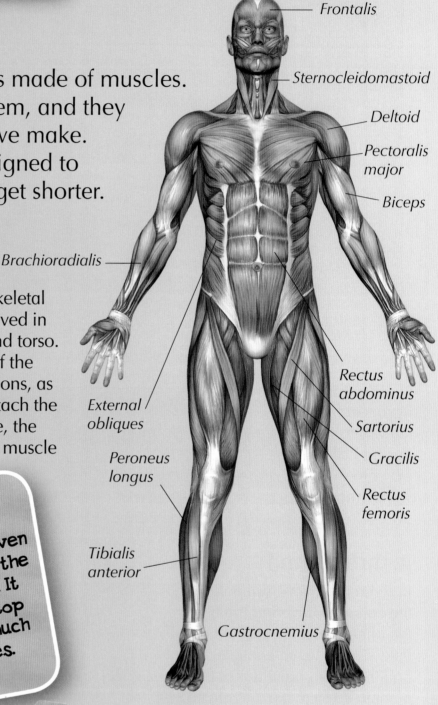

Frontalis

Sternocleidomastoid

Deltoid

Pectoralis major

Biceps

Brachioradialis

Rectus abdominus

External obliques

Sartorius

Gracilis

Peroneus longus

Rectus femoris

Tibialis anterior

Gastrocnemius

It's Amazing!

The smallest muscle is not even as big as this 'i'. It is called the stapedius inside the ear. It pulls the ear bones to stop them from shaking too much during very loud noises.

Biceps

More muscles?

Bodybuilders who exercise to build up their muscles don't have more muscles than anyone else. Each muscle just becomes bigger and bulges more under the skin.

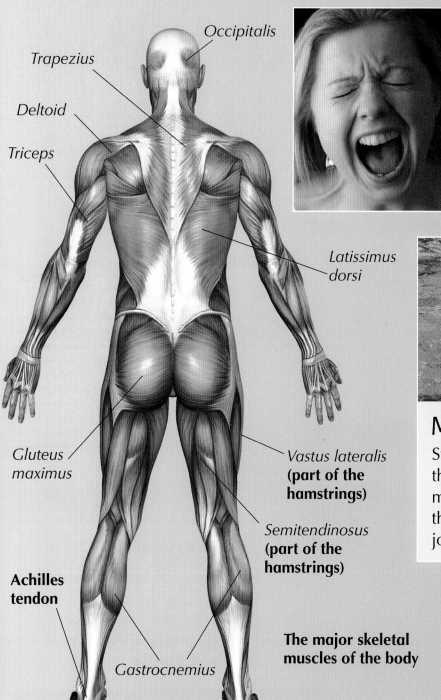

Occipitalis

Trapezius

Deltoid

Triceps

Latissimus dorsi

Gluteus maximus

Vastus lateralis **(part of the hamstrings)**

Semitendinosus **(part of the hamstrings)**

Achilles tendon

Gastrocnemius

The major skeletal muscles of the body

Noise muscles

Your skeletal muscles are also involved in some small, less obvious actions. For example, when you talk or shout, the breathing muscles push out air from the lungs and through the voice box.

Muscle support

Swimming is especially good for the muscles and joints. It exercises muscles that are rarely used, and the water supports the body so the joints do not get injured.

Muscle names

Some of the body's muscles have scientific names, and a few of these have become well known. The *pectoralis major* muscles, or pectorals, are in the upper chest. The *rectus abdominus* muscles, or abdominals, are in the front of the abdomen. The biceps is the bulging muscle in the upper arm. The hamstrings is the common name given to the strong muscles at the rear of the thigh.

Top Facts

- **The body has about 650 muscles.**
- **The biggest muscle is the *gluteus maximus* in the buttock.**
- **The longest muscle is the *sartorius* muscle. It runs down the front of the upper leg.**

Inside a muscle

Each muscle is made up of thousands of tiny strands, called muscle fibres, that are about as thick as a hair. The muscles also have blood vessels to bring plenty of blood. The blood carries nutrients, which the muscles use to power their movement.

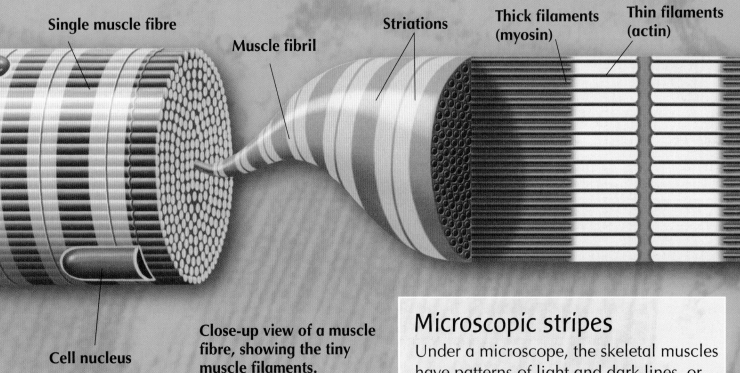

Single muscle fibre

Muscle fibril

Striations

Thick filaments (myosin)

Thin filaments (actin)

Cell nucleus

Close-up view of a muscle fibre, showing the tiny muscle filaments.

Microscopic stripes

Under a microscope, the skeletal muscles have patterns of light and dark lines, or striations. These form where groups of thick and thin filaments – myosin and actin – overlap each other.

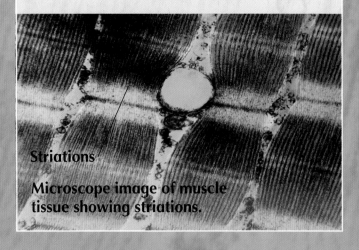

Striations

Microscope image of muscle tissue showing striations.

Smaller and smaller

There are thousands of muscle fibres in a big muscle, such as the ones in the leg. Each fibre is made of thinner threads, known as muscle fibrils. And each fibril contains even thinner strands, or filaments, of two substances – actin and myosin. These substances are proteins, and they move to make the muscles shorter.

Sliding past

A muscle is controlled by nerve signals from the brain. When the signals arrive, they make the strands of actin and myosin slide past each other. As they do so, they shorten the fibril, which in turn, shortens the fibre and the whole muscle. Most muscles can shorten to about two-thirds their relaxed length.

It's Amazing!

The body's bendiest muscle is the one you use to talk, eat, drink and lick your lips. It's your tongue!

In this tug-of-war game, the muscles in the arms and legs are being stretched rather than shortened.

Taking the strain

Muscles usually work by shortening and pulling the bones. They can also stretch in order to pull against something else, such as a rope. This type of muscle use is called isometric, which means 'same length'.

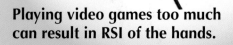

Playing video games too much can result in RSI of the hands.

Wear and tear

Muscles, tendons, nerves and joints that repeat the same movement may suffer damage. This can result in pain known as repetitive strain injury, or RSI. RSI happens most commonly in the hands – often in the hand used to control a computer mouse.

Finger control

- Hold out your hand so that the fingers are together and straight.
- Then, curl your fingers all at the same time, as though you are gripping something.
- Now, try to curl each finger on its own, while keeping the others straight.
- It's more difficult to curl one finger at a time because your brain has to learn to send the correct nerve signals to control the muscles in each finger.

How muscles work

Every movement needs muscles – not just jumping or lifting something heavy, but simple actions that we do all the time, such as blinking and breathing.

Shorten and stretch

A muscle can pull, but it cannot push. This means that a single muscle can only move a bone in one direction. Another muscle is needed in order to pull a bone in the opposite direction. Many muscles are arranged as opposite partners, like this, working together to pull bones one way and then the other.

Muscle matters

- The word 'muscle' comes from the Latin word 'musculus', meaning 'little mouse', because in the past people thought that bulging muscles looked like a mouse running under the skin!
- The first accurate pictures of the whole muscle system were drawn by the artist and scientist Andreas Vesalius in 1543.

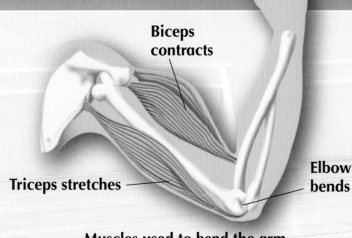

Biceps contracts

Triceps stretches

Elbow bends

Muscles used to bend the arm.

Triceps contracts

Biceps stretches

Muscles used to straighten the arm.

Elbow straightens

Opposing partners

The main muscles in the upper arm are the biceps and triceps. When the biceps contracts, it pulls the lower arm up. This makes the elbow bend and relaxes the triceps. When the triceps contracts, or gets shorter, it pulls the lower arm down. This straightens the elbow and stretches the biceps. The triceps and biceps are examples of muscles that work as antagonistic, or opposing, partners.

Working together

Apart from very simple actions such as blinking, few movements use just one or two muscles. As you write your name, your finger muscles hold the pen, and your hand and wrist muscles move the pen to form the words. Your arm and shoulder muscles move your whole arm along the page, and your eye, head and neck muscles move so you can watch what you write. More than 100 muscles are involved!

A crane uses cables to pull and lift heavy loads.

Pulling force

A crane's lifting cable works in a similar way to a muscle. It lifts the load, or pulls it up, by shortening the cable as it winds onto a spool.

It's Amazing!

The widest muscles in your body are the external obliques, which run from the middle of your back and around to your stomach. They can measure up to 45 centimetres wide.

Learning muscles

Learning to use muscles together can take a lot of time. Movements that you find easy today, such as walking, may have taken you 12 months to learn as a baby.

A ballet dancer using the muscles in her legs to stand on points, or tiptoe.

Making faces

Did you know that we can communicate without saying a single word! The muscles in our faces can make a lot of small or large movements, pulling parts of the face and allowing us to show a vast range of feelings, moods and emotions.

Expressions

The face has more than 60 muscles. We use them all the time, often without realizing it. As people look at us, our faces show what we are thinking and feeling. We can try to hide our facial expressions for a time, but it's hard to fake them for long. Actors learn to control their facial expressions when they pretend to have certain feelings and emotions.

Pulling faces

The facial muscles are at different angles to each other. They can pull the skin, lips, cheeks and other features into a great many positions. For example, the eyebrows are raised by contracting the *frontalis* muscle that runs vertically along the forehead. It is also used to make the forehead frown.

A girl using her face muscles to create a funny face.

The major muscles of the face with their scientific names

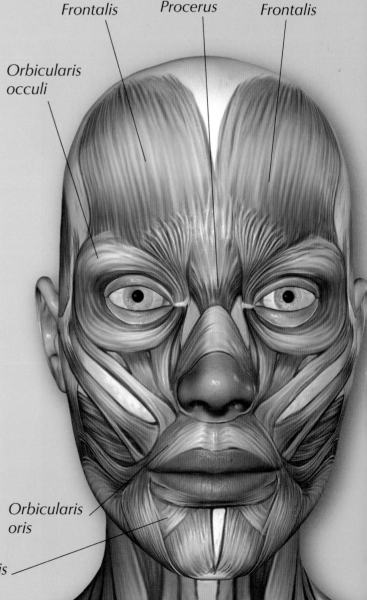

Frontalis *Procerus* *Frontalis*

Orbicularis occuli

Orbicularis oris

Depressor labii inferioris

Facial emotions

- Look in a mirror and watch your eyebrows closely.
- Raise them high and you look surprised.
- Lower them slightly and you look puzzled.
- Lower them more and you look annoyed.
- Now, bring them really low and you look very angry.

'Smiling' chimp

Many animals, such as chimps, seem to smile, but we must be careful not to assume that their expressions are the same as ours. In fact, a chimp bares its teeth, or 'smiles', when it is afraid and ready to defend itself.

A chimp 'smiles' to show fear.

The major muscles of the side of the head with their scientific names

Frontalis

Orbicularis occuli

Temporalis

Nasalis

Occipitalis

Masseter

Levator labii superioris

Orbicularis oris

Risorius

Zygomaticus major

Sternocleidomastoid

Facial muscles

Most muscles are joined to bones, but in the face, the muscles are joined to each other or to the skin. They contract by tiny amounts, making other muscles nearby stretch. When the muscles do this, they move the skin and make the facial features, such as the eyebrows and lips, move. All of this produces a facial expression.

It's Amazing!

It's easier to smile than to frown! A happy smile uses less than 20 face muscles. A sad frown needs twice as many. Save energy and smile!

Other types of muscle

The skeletal muscles are not the body's only muscles. The heart has its own type of muscle, and the gut, blood vessels and many other parts have a kind of muscle called smooth muscle.

Never tires

If we use some muscles too much, they become tired and weak, but one type of muscle never tires. It is the cardiac muscle that makes up the walls of the heart, and it works every second of every day to pump blood around the body. The walls of the blood vessels contain smooth muscles, which alter the width of these tubes to control how much blood flows to different body parts.

It's Amazing!

Usually the muscles in the stomach and guts work smoothly, but if we have a fright or feel worried, these muscles can suddenly shorten. We feel this as a fluttering – known as 'butterflies' – in our stomach.

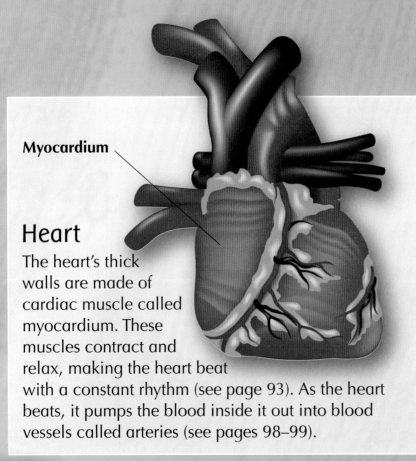

Myocardium

Heart

The heart's thick walls are made of cardiac muscle called myocardium. These muscles contract and relax, making the heart beat with a constant rhythm (see page 93). As the heart beats, it pumps the blood inside it out into blood vessels called arteries (see pages 98–99).

Top Facts

Smooth muscles are found in the walls of many parts of the body including:

- The oesophagus, or foodpipe.
- The stomach.
- The intestines.
- The blood vessels.
- The windpipe.
- The airways in the lungs called bronchi and bronchioles (see pages 70–71).
- The ureters – the tubes that carry urine from the kidneys to the bladder.
- The bladder.

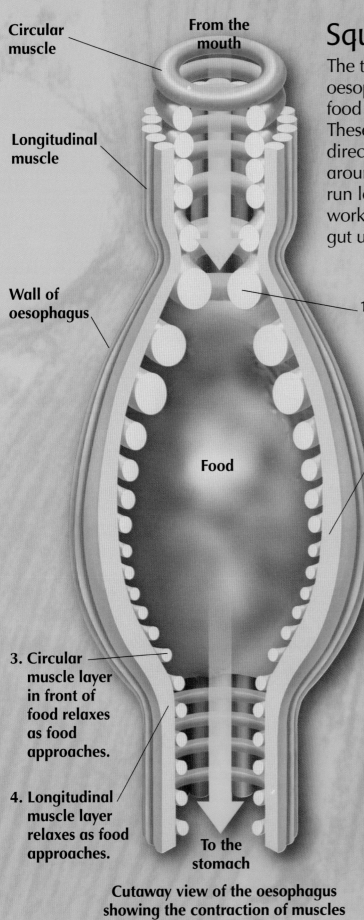

Circular muscle

From the mouth

Longitudinal muscle

Wall of oesophagus

Food

3. Circular muscle layer in front of food relaxes as food approaches.

4. Longitudinal muscle layer relaxes as food approaches.

To the stomach

Cutaway view of the oesophagus showing the contraction of muscles during peristalsis.

Squeezing food

The tube-shaped walls of the gut – the oesophagus, stomach and intestines – push food through them using smooth muscles. These smooth muscles are arranged in two directions. The circular muscles form rings around the gut and the longitudinal muscles run lengthways along the gut. These layers work together to squeeze the food through the gut using a wave action called peristalsis.

1. Circular muscle layer behind food contracts to push food forwards.

2. Longitudinal muscle layer contracts to shorten tube.

Automatic journey

We bite, chew and swallow using muscles in the face and neck that we control. Once the food gets into the oesphagus, the automatic movements of the smooth muscles take over to take food down into the stomach and through the intestines (see pages 112–137).

Bone, joint and muscle problems

Overexerting ourselves or putting too much pressure on our bones, joints and muscles can cause breaks, strains or tears that may require medical treatment.

Muscle cramp

During hard exercise, a chemical called lactic acid builds up in the muscles. This is usually carried away by the blood. However, if too little blood reaches the muscle to flush away the lactic acid, the muscle could develop cramp. This is an uncontrolled contraction, or tightening, known as a spasm, and is very painful.

The football player on the ground has developed cramp, so his teammate is stretching his legs to relieve the pain.

Top Facts

- A muscle strain is when a muscle pulls too hard and damages some of its fibres.

- A muscle tear is like a strain but the muscle fibres split.

- A joint sprain is when a joint moves too far and its parts become swollen, stiff and painful.

It's Amazing!

Some headaches are caused by problems with muscles. Tension headaches are the result of spasms in the neck muscles, which restrict the flow of blood to the head.

New hip

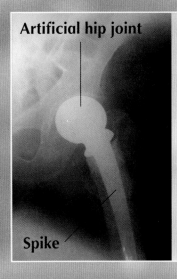

Artificial hip joint

Spike

This X-ray shows an artificial hip joint (see page 45). The ball-shaped end of the thigh bone has been replaced with a metal one and fixed into the thigh bone with a spike.

Breaks

A break in a bone is called a fracture. It may be a slight crack or a complete snap. An X-ray tells the doctor if the bone is fractured. If it is, the doctor may push the broken bone back together. The bone may be held in place by a plaster or fibreglass cast as it mends.

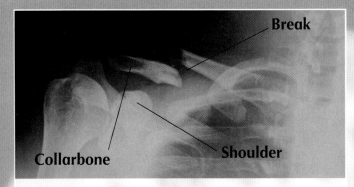

Break

Collarbone **Shoulder**

Broken collarbone

A broken collarbone, as shown in this X-ray, is often caused by falling and putting out a straight arm to prevent the head from hitting the ground. The force of the fall passes from the arm to the shoulder and snaps the collarbone.

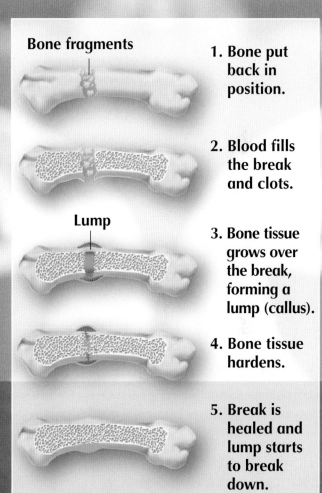

Bone fragments

Lump

1. Bone put back in position.

2. Blood fills the break and clots.

3. Bone tissue grows over the break, forming a lump (callus).

4. Bone tissue hardens.

5. Break is healed and lump starts to break down.

Healing a break

The body takes about six weeks to mend a broken bone, depending on how bad the break is. Blood fills the break and new bone tissue grows in the gap. This gradually hardens to form a permanent, strong repair.

Healthy bones and joints

Bones, joints and muscles are meant to be used, and exercise can help them to stay healthy. You should also eat a good diet so that these body parts can stay strong and active, and repair themselves if they get damaged.

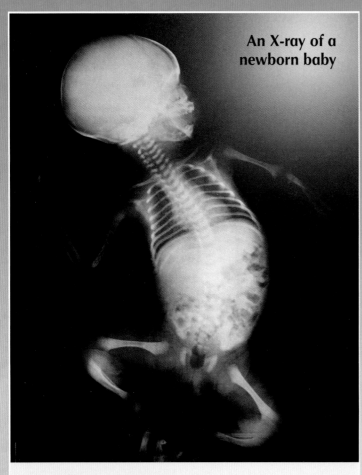

An X-ray of a newborn baby

Keeping active

We need to use our bones, joints and muscles often or they will weaken and waste away. As well as sports, there are helpful things we can do as part of our daily lives. We can walk or cycle rather than travel by car and use the stairs rather than lifts – all of these small actions add up to keep our bodies healthy.

Baby skeleton

As a baby develops in the womb, its skeleton first forms from cartilage. The cartilage gradually turns into bone, and this process – known as ossification – continues during childhood. The whole skeleton is not fully grown, mature and hardened until a person has reached about 20 years of age.

It's Amazing!

Improvements in muscle training methods and diet mean that a modern champion runner can finish the 100 metres sprint almost one second faster than a champion runner of 100 years ago.

Warm up, cool down

Sports people and athletes know the importance of proper training. If the body tries to do too much too quickly, it can suffer injuries, such as sprains and strains. Before you start exercising, it's important to get expert advice. You should also do warm-up exercises, such as bending and stretching, before a sudden burst of activity and cool-down exercises afterwards to help the body relax again.

Healthy bones

Bones and teeth contain large amounts of the mineral calcium. Milk and other dairy products are rich in calcium. If they are taken during childhood, they help the bones and teeth to grow well and strong.

This runner is stretching her leg muscles before starting to exercise.

Top Facts

- Some people are naturally fitter and better at sports and exercise than other people. You should aim to improve your own performance rather than try to match someone else's.

- You should exercise steadily and take guidance from a coach.

- It is important to have the correct equipment, especially footwear.

- You should wear the correct body protection and guards for contact sports, such as rugby.

LUNGS AND BREATHING

In an emergency, your body can make do without food for several days, and it can even cope without water for a day or so. But one thing is so vital that your body cannot survive more than a few minutes without it – the gas oxygen. You take in oxygen from the air around you by breathing, using the parts of the body called the respiratory system. You don't have to think about breathing – your body does it automatically – but it keeps you alive.

The breathing system

The respiratory, or breathing, system is located in the head, neck and chest. You use it to draw air deep into your lungs. Here, oxygen passes into the blood and then spreads all around your body.

The main parts of the respiratory system in the neck and chest

Bigger and smaller

The lungs act like two balloons inside your chest. As you draw air into the breathing system (see pages 76–77), the lungs get bigger as they fill with air. Then when you breathe out, air is pushed out of the lungs and they get smaller.

The airways

The upper airways in the head and neck include the throat and the nasal chamber inside the nose (see page 64). The lower airways include the windpipe in the neck and the tubes called bronchi and bronchioles, which carry air into the lungs. At the top of the windpipe is the larynx, or voice box, which produces the voice when air passes through it.

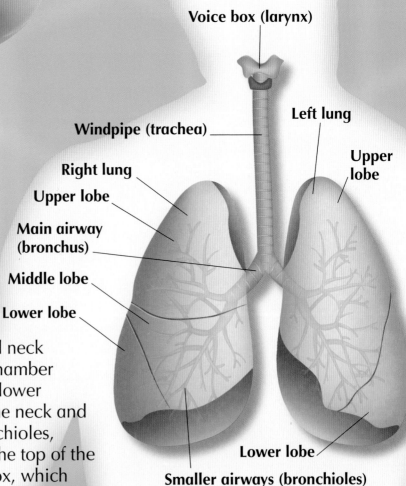

Voice box (larynx)

Windpipe (trachea)

Left lung

Upper lobe

Right lung

Upper lobe

Main airway (bronchus)

Middle lobe

Lower lobe

Lower lobe

Smaller airways (bronchioles)

Fanning the flames

In ancient times, many people thought that body warmth came from food being burned in the heart. They believed that breathing was a way of providing air for the burning flames in the heart. They thought that when the body was active, breathing increased to provide more air to fan the flames, making the body hotter.

Down into the lungs

The breathing muscles create the movement that sucks air in and pushes air out of your lungs. The most important muscles are the dome-shaped diaphragm below the lungs and the long muscles between the ribs called intercostals. The backbone, ribs and breastbone form a cage around the lungs, which protects these parts yet still allows the breathing action (see pages 76-77).

It's Amazing!

A free diver is someone who dives underwater without an air tank. Some free divers can hold their breath for more than 6 minutes when they dive.

Sense of smell

Air coming in through the nose carries tiny particles of smell chemicals. These particles land on sensitive patches in the roof of the nasal chamber. The patches work out the type of particle and send information about the smell to the brain (see pages 174–175).

Blowing

In normal breathing, air flows in and out through the nose, but the air flow can be directed out through the mouth. This is useful for all kinds of actions, from blowing out candles to playing the trumpet.

Inside the nose

Most air is breathed in through the nose. Inside the nose, air is cleaned, warmed and moistened to make it more suitable for travelling into the lungs. Dusty, cold or dry air can clog the lungs or dry out the airways.

Air filters

The nose is separated into two nostrils by a wall of cartilage (see pages 44–45). The nostrils have small hairs inside them that catch bits of dust and other particles floating in the air. The nostrils are the entrance to the nasal cavity, an air-filled space that works like an air filter. The lining of the nasal cavity is coated with a layer of mucus, a thick, sticky fluid that moistens the air and traps germs, dust and other particles.

An X-ray of the skull showing the nasal cavity and the sinuses.

Frontal sinus

Ethmoid and sphenoid sinuses

Maxillary sinus

Nasal cavity

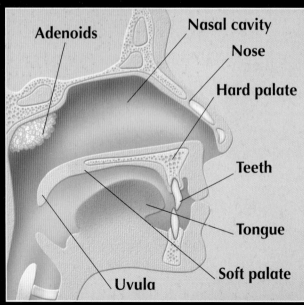

Adenoids

Nasal cavity

Nose

Hard palate

Teeth

Tongue

Soft palate

Uvula

Nasal cavity

The nasal cavity is separated from the mouth by the palate, which is divided into the hard, bony palate at the front and the soft palate at the back. The adenoids are bulges of tissue that help to trap and remove germs from air.

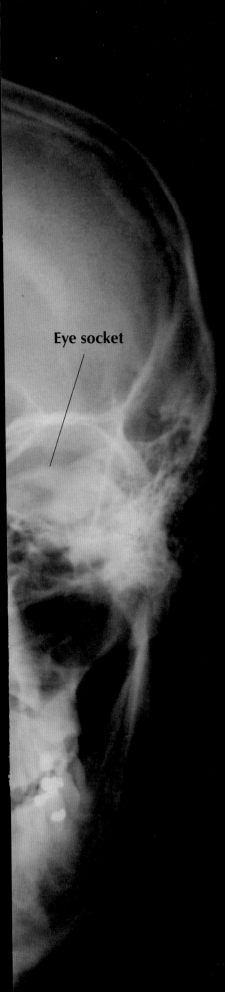

Eye socket

Top Facts

- Branching off the nasal cavity are a number of air-filled spaces called sinuses.

- There are four sets of sinuses in the skull. These are the frontal, ethmoid, sphenoid and maxillary sinuses.

- No-one knows exactly what the sinuses are for, but they may be used to help make the different sounds of speech, or to help with temperature control within the head, or to make the bones of the skull lighter.

Synchronized swimmers wearing nose clips.

Closed nose

Synchronized swimmers usually wear a nose clip when they are performing. This stops water entering the nasal cavity and irritating the cavity lining, especially when the swimmers are upside down in the pool.

Warmed by blood

The nasal cavity has a thin lining with a network of blood vessels just beneath the surface. The warm blood flowing through these vessels gives out heat to the passing air, warming the air. These blood vessels are delicate – a knock to the nose may break one and cause a nosebleed.

Face masks

People with certain jobs, such as builders and miners, wear masks with filters. These masks stop dust particles, which the nasal cavity cannot trap, from entering the breathing system, where they might cause damage.

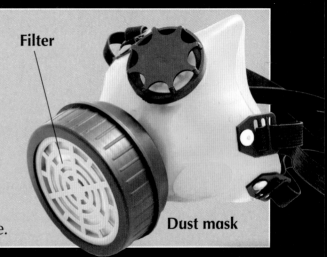

Filter

Dust mask

In the throat

The throat has two functions – it is a passageway for air and for food. Swallowing closes off the windpipe, so food is not accidentally carried into the lower airways.

The right way

When you swallow, the entrance to the windpipe tilts up and forwards and a stiff flap – the epiglottis – tilts down over it. This piece of cartilage blocks the upper entrance to your windpipe, which means that food slides down into the oesophagus. It is not possible to breathe when swallowing because the windpipe is closed.

When we eat, as these women are, we do not usually think about the action of swallowing – we just do it.

It's Amazing!

On average, a person swallows 300 times during a meal and up to 2000 times during a whole day.

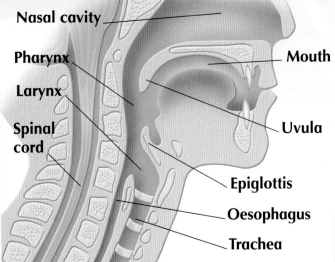

Nasal cavity

Pharynx

Larynx

Spinal cord

Mouth

Uvula

Epiglottis

Oesophagus

Trachea

Open wide

The throat connects your mouth and nasal cavity to your trachea, or windpipe, and the oesophagus, which is a tube down to the stomach. The upper part of the throat is called the pharynx. Below this is the larynx, or voice box, which is the opening to the respiratory tract. At the sides of the throat there are bulges of special germ-killing tissue called the tonsils, which, like the adenoids, help to fight infection.

Swollen tonsils

The tonsils may swell when they are fighting germs in the body, causing a sore throat and discomfort when swallowing. This illness is called tonsillitis.

Tonsils

A child with infected tonsils

The wrong way

Very rarely, swallowed food may go down 'the wrong way'. This means it goes into the windpipe and blocks the airway. If this happens, breathing becomes difficult and can even stop, causing choking. Usually a cough removes the blockage by forcing fast-moving air up from the lungs. This blows the food up into the throat for safe swallowing.

Choking

If coughing cannot remove an obstruction from the windpipe, then a trained person may have to perform the Heimlich manoeuvre. This other person squeezes the lower chest to press the lungs, which forces air and the blockage out.

Heimlich manoeuvre

Blockage is forced out of the windpipe.

Arms squeeze the lower chest.

Voice box and speaking

The larynx, or voice box, is at the top of the trachea, or windpipe. In men and some women, it can be seen as a hard bulge at the front of the neck, which is called the Adam's apple. The larynx allows us to make vocalizations, or sounds – these can range from a quiet whisper to a loud shout.

This opera singer has learned how to control her vocal cords to produce beautiful sounds.

Vocal cords

Sticking out from the inside of your voice box are two flap-like strips that look like ridges (see below). These are your vocal cords. In normal breathing, the vocal cords are held apart by muscles. This forms a V-shaped gap between them, which is known as the glottis. Air passes silently through the glottis when you are breathing normally.

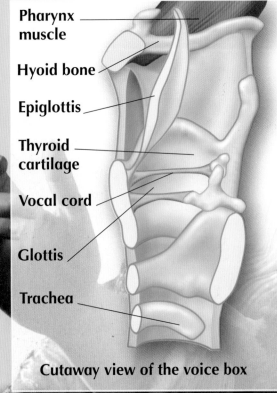

Pharynx muscle
Hyoid bone
Epiglottis
Thyroid cartilage
Vocal cord
Glottis
Trachea

Cutaway view of the voice box

Voice box

The voice box is made of nine curved plates of cartilage (see pages 44–45). The main cartilage plate is the thyroid cartilage. These plates help to keep the voice box open. There are also muscles connected to these cartilage plates. The muscles move the plates to change the shape of the vocal cords and the size of the glottis.

Top Facts

- Women's voices are usually higher than men's because their vocal cords are shorter and vibrate more quickly.

- Men's vocal cords range between 17–25 millimetres long, while women's vocal cords are just 12.5–17.5 millimetres in length.

Vocal sounds

The wide range of sounds you can make with your voice are controlled by the vibration of the vocal cords. When the muscles pull on your vocal cords, they make the gap between the cords narrower. Air flowing from the lungs through this narrow gap makes the cords vibrate, or shake fast. This produces the basic sounds of the voice. The sounds are altered and made louder by the air spaces in the mouth, the nose and the sinuses. The shapes of these spaces vary from person to person, which is why each of us has a unique and individual voice.

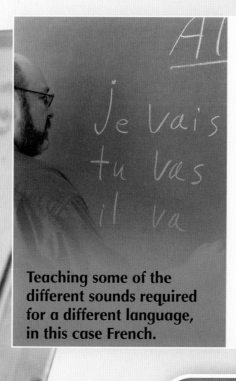

Teaching some of the different sounds required for a different language, in this case French.

Pronunciation

You use your tongue, cheeks and mouth to speak the words you use every day. When you learn a new language, you may have to learn how to make completely new sounds. To do this, you will have to create new shapes with your mouth, cheeks, teeth and tongue so that you can pronounce foreign words correctly.

Speaking while breathing

- The vocal cords only work properly with air that is being breathed out.

- Test this by speaking while breathing in. It's much harder than speaking normally, and the sounds seem to disappear into your chest.

Lower airways

The lower airways carry breathed-in air down through the neck and into the lungs. There, the airways divide many times, becoming smaller and smaller as they carry air into the deepest parts of the lungs.

Airway tree

The system of branching airways is often compared to an upside-down tree. The main 'trunk' is the trachea, or windpipe. This divides into two main airway 'branches', the left bronchus and right bronchus. These bronchi split over and over again. They first form secondary bronchi, and then split to become smaller and smaller until they eventually become the smallest airways, known as bronchioles, which are the tree's 'twigs' (see pages 72–73).

Top Facts

- In an average adult, the windpipe is about 12 centimetres long. Its width, or diameter, inside measures about 1.5 centimetres.

- When we breathe in deeply or crane our neck to look up and forwards, the windpipe can stretch in length by up to 3 centimetres.

Cutaway view of trachea and oesophagus

Voice box (larynx)

Cartilage rings

Windpipe (trachea)

Right bronchus

Right secondary bronchi

Left bronchus

Left secondary bronchi

The windpipe

The windpipe starts at the base of the larynx, or voice box. Its walls are formed of 16 to 20 C-shaped rings of cartilage. These allow the windpipe to stretch, twist and shorten as the neck moves, yet remain open for air to flow through it.

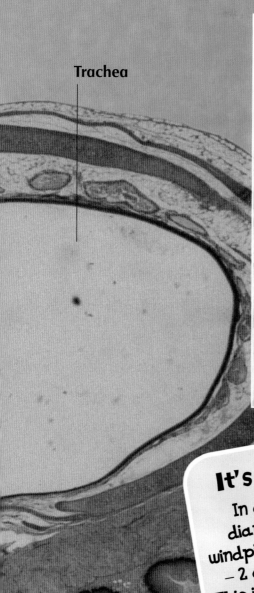

Trachea

Oesophagus

Inside the trachea

The trachea and the oesophagus run side by side down the neck (see main image). The C-shaped rings of cartilage that surround the trachea allow it to squash slightly if a large piece of food passes down the oesophagus.

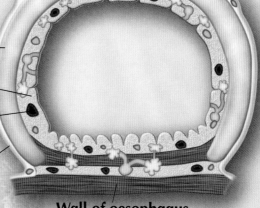

Cartilage C-ring

Lining of trachea

Small artery

Outer wall

Wall of oesophagus

It's Amazing!

In a baby, the diameter of the windpipe is very small – 2 or 3 millimetres. This is not much wider than the ink tube inside a typical ballpoint pen.

Keeping clean

The windpipe and other airways are lined with a sticky fluid called mucus, or phlegm. This traps bits of dirt and germs floating in the breathed-in air. The mucus is made continuously by microscopic cells called goblet cells in the airway lining. Coughing brings mucus up from the airways into the throat, where it can be swallowed (see page 79).

Cilia on the lining of the airway

Tiny hairs

Microscopic hairs called cilia stick out from the lining of the airways. They wave continuously to push mucus up the airways.

Deep in the lungs

The lungs are like elastic bags filled with millions of tiny balloons. In each lung, the branching airways become thinner and shorter until, finally, after about 15 divisions from the windpipe, they are narrower than human hairs.

The lungs

Each lung is made up of sections called lobes (see page 62), and each lobe has a bronchus leading to it. The right lung has three lobes – upper, middle and lower. The left lung is smaller and has only two lobes – upper and lower – because it has a scooped-out area where the heart sits. The oesophagus and the main blood vessels lie between the lungs.

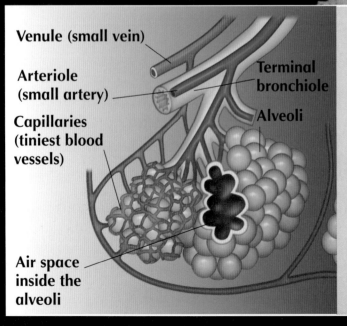

Venule (small vein)

Arteriole (small artery)

Capillaries (tiniest blood vessels)

Terminal bronchiole

Alveoli

Air space inside the alveoli

Into the blood

The smallest airways, called the terminal bronchioles, carry air to groups of microscopic, bubble-shaped air sacs called alveoli. The alveoli are surrounded by plenty of blood vessels so that oxygen can pass easily from the lungs and into the blood (see page 74).

A resin cast showing the smaller and smaller airways inside the lungs.

- Each lung has about 300 million alveoli.
- Each alveolus is about 0.2 millimetres in diameter.
- The name alveolus comes from the Latin word meaning 'little cavity'.
- If spread out, the millions of alveoli in a pair of lungs would cover the area of a tennis court.

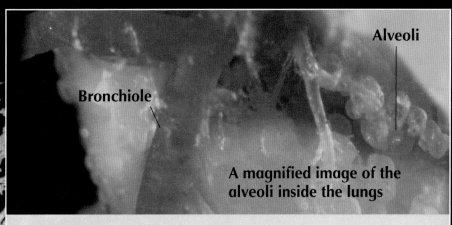

Bronchiole

Alveoli

A magnified image of the alveoli inside the lungs

Alveoli

Under a microscope, alveoli look like small, almost see-through balloons. Most alveoli are not separate from each other but are squashed together so that they look like bunches of grapes. As a result of this, they are partly merged inside and have one large, shared air space.

Into the blood

Oxygen from breathed-in air passes into the body through the alveoli. It seeps from the air in the alveoli into the blood in the microscopic blood vessels, known as capillaries, around the alveoli. This is also where the waste gas carbon dioxide moves from the blood into the alveoli and is eventually breathed out.

It's Amazing!

The lungs are the only part of the body that could float on water. In fact, people float more easily on water if they breathe in deeply, and then take small breaths, keeping the lungs as full of air as possible.

Fair exchange

Breathing involves an exchange – vital oxygen is taken into the body and swapped for waste carbon dioxide, which is removed. This is known as respiratory gas exchange.

Thin barrier

A very thin barrier separates the air inside the alveoli from the blood in the capillaries around them. This barrier is made up of the wall of each alveolus and the wall of each capillary. The blood in the capillaries is low in oxygen, so oxygen passes through the barrier into the blood. As the red cells absorb oxygen, the blood changes from a dark bluish-red colour to bright red.

It's Amazing!

The barrier formed by the wall of the capillary and the alveolus together is about 100 times thinner than the paper of this page.

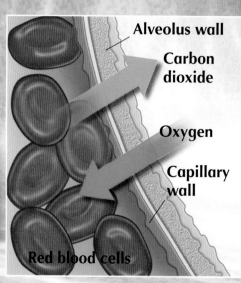

Alveolus wall

Carbon dioxide

Oxygen

Capillary wall

Red blood cells

Gas swap

As oxygen passes into the blood, it is absorbed by billions of red blood cells. These carry oxygen around the body to where it is needed. At the same time, carbon dioxide passes from the blood and into the air in the lungs.

Underwater problem

As well as in the air, oxygen is found dissolved in water. Human lungs and airways can take oxygen from air but not from water. So when people are underwater, they have to hold their breath and survive on the oxygen held in their lungs for as long as they can. When the body is more active or exercising, it needs more oxygen and makes more waste carbon dioxide, so it must breathe faster and deeper. This is why we run out of breath so quickly when swimming underwater.

Young babies naturally hold their breath when swimming underwater.

First look

The tiny alveoli and capillaries could not be seen before the invention of the microscope. In 1661, Italian scientist Marcello Malpighi looked at magnified images of the lungs and saw the capillaries. His discovery allowed people to understand how oxygen moves from the air into the blood.

Submarine

Inside a submarine, the crew breathe the same air for days, weeks or even months. Air cleaners, filters and fresheners remove carbon dioxide and other waste from the air and add fresh oxygen.

A submarine on the surface before diving under water.

The mudskipper fish appears to breathe when out of the water.

Mudskipper

Fish get oxygen from water using special organs called gills. The mudskipper spends some time out of the water and seems to breathe air. But really its gills store water and take oxygen from it. When the oxygen runs out, the fish returns to the water.

Movements of breathing

The actions of the main breathing muscles – the intercostals and the diaphragm – are carried out automatically. As a result, you do not have to think about breathing in and out for most of the time.

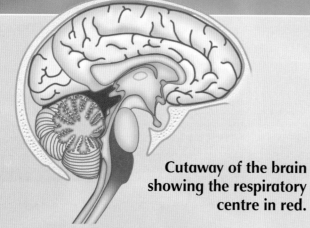

Cutaway of the brain showing the respiratory centre in red.

Breathing control

The breathing muscles are controlled by signals from a part of the brain called the respiratory centre. This detects the amounts of oxygen and carbon dioxide in the blood. As carbon dioxide levels rise and oxygen levels fall, the brain tells the breathing muscles to work harder.

Breathing in

To inhale, or breathe in, the diaphragm contracts, becoming flatter. This pulls the lungs downwards. At the same time, the intercostals contract and make the ribs move up and out. The result is that the lungs are stretched and suck air in through the nose and down the windpipe into the chest.

It's Amazing!

At rest, about half a litre of air flows in and out of the lungs in each breath. After exercise, breathing is faster, and the amount of air that flows in and out of the lungs every minute is about 20 times more than at rest.

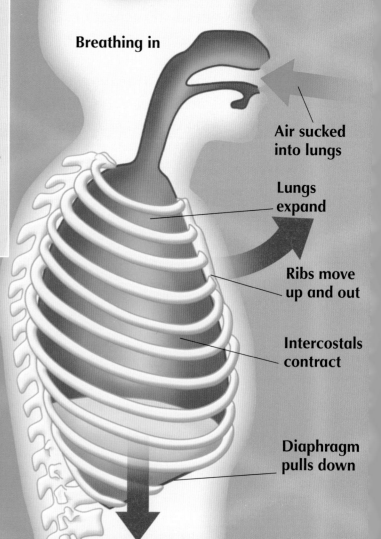

Breathing in

Air sucked into lungs

Lungs expand

Ribs move up and out

Intercostals contract

Diaphragm pulls down

Breathing rate

- Rest for a few minutes, then count how many breaths you take in 1 minute. Then jog on the spot for 3 minutes, and count your breaths.

- Rest again, then count your breaths. Your breathing rate should rise after activity, then gradually return to its resting rate.

A boy holds his breath while jumping into water.

Breathing out

To exhale, or breathe out, the diaphragm and the intercostals all relax. The lungs, which have stretched like an elastic band, spring back to their usual shape. This makes the diaphragm return to its dome shape and the ribs move down and in. As the lungs shrink, they push air up the windpipe and out through the nose.

Stop breathing

We have to make ourselves stop breathing when we jump into water. The brain tries to make us breathe, but we can prevent it for a while so our lungs are not filled with water.

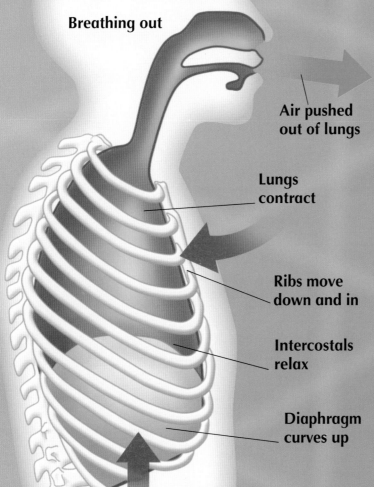

Breathing out

Air pushed out of lungs

Lungs contract

Ribs move down and in

Intercostals relax

Diaphragm curves up

Mouth-to-mouth

Breathed-out air still contains some oxygen. It can be blown into someone's lungs in an emergency if he or she has stopped breathing. This is called artificial respiration.

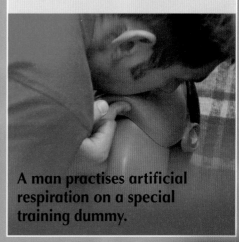
A man practises artificial respiration on a special training dummy.

Coughs and sneezes

Potentially harmful substances in the air are sometimes breathed into the lungs. Fortunately, the body has ways of protecting itself from these foreign invaders, and can get rid of them at super-fast speeds.

Sneezing

Small particles of dust that get into the nose may irritate the nose lining. This produces the sneeze reflex. Muscles in the chest, the diaphragm (see page 76) and the throat contract – or get smaller – very quickly. This forces air up through the nose, carrying the cause of the irritation and mucus with it.

Sneezing can be caused by tiny plant particles called pollen. This is known as hay fever (see page 82).

Top Facts

- You always close your eyes when you sneeze.

- A typical sneeze will blow about 40,000 tiny droplets of mucus and saliva out of the nose and mouth.

- The droplets blown out by coughs and sneezes may contain germs. This is why it is important to cover your mouth and nose.

Airway irritation

If an irritation occurs lower down the breathing system, such as in the trachea or the lungs, then the body produces a cough to clear it. The irritation may be caused by small particles of dust or it might be caused by an illness that inflames the linings of the lower airways.

Always put your hand over your mouth when coughing to stop the spread of germs.

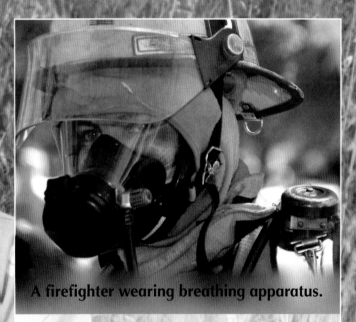

A firefighter wearing breathing apparatus.

Dust and smoke protection

People who work in dusty or smoky places need to wear protection to stop dangerous particles from entering the breathing system. In some cases, this protection can be a simple mask, which blocks larger dust particles (see page 65). However, in very smoky environments, such as a fire, a person may need to carry a supply of dust-free air.

Coughing

To cope with an irritation in the airways, the lining of the breathing passages produces excessive mucus. The body coughs to get rid of this excessive mucus. As with a sneeze, a cough is caused by a sudden contraction of the muscles in the chest, which forces air out of the lungs as well as the excess mucus and the cause of the irritation.

It's Amazing!
Sneezes blow air out of the nose at speeds of up to 150 kilometres per hour!

Nose and throat problems

Breathing difficulties may be caused by physical problems with the structure of the respiratory, or breathing, system. This can lead to a variety of conditions, such as snoring.

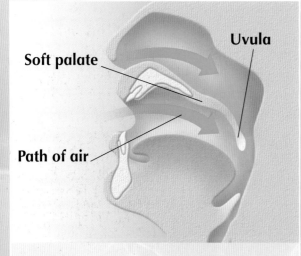

Soft palate

Uvula

Path of air

Snoring

Snoring is caused by the vibration of soft parts at the back of the throat, such as the soft palate and the flap that hangs down at the back of the mouth, called the uvula. These parts vibrate as air passes over them when a person is asleep. This noisy vibration can keep other people awake. Snoring can be caused by a variety of conditions, such as fat gathering around the throat, a blockage of the nose passages or a weakness of the throat muscles.

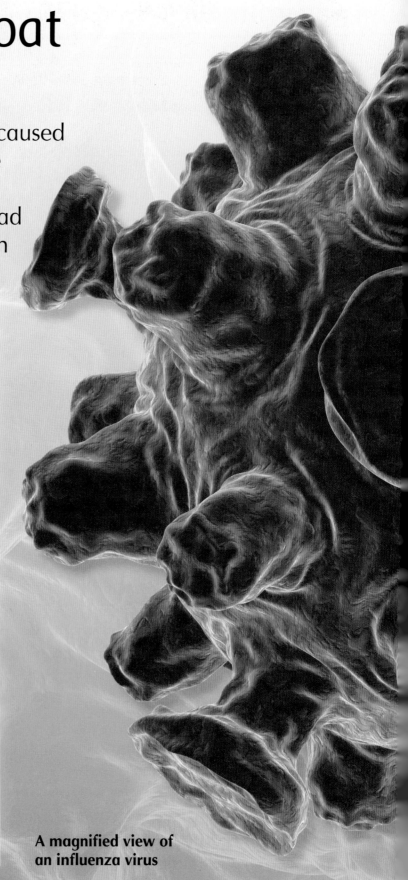

A magnified view of an influenza virus

Dangerous substances

The respiratory system can be damaged by substances in the air. These can include tiny organisms, such as other viruses and germs that cause illnesses like colds and influenza. They can also be chemicals that the body cannot get rid of by coughing and that can damage the body's tissues.

It's Amazing!

The loudest recorded snore measured 93 decibels – that's louder than the sound of a pneumatic drill breaking up concrete.

A microscopic view of asbestos fibres

Asbestos

Asbestos is a flame-resistant material that was used in buildings until the 1980s. It was then discovered that the tiny strands that make up some kinds of asbestos could cause cancer when breathed in. As a result, asbestos is banned in many countries, and any found in old buildings has to be disposed of very carefully.

Smog

Smog is a cloud of potentially harmful gas that is formed when sunlight reacts with polluting gases from car exhausts and factories. Smog can cause soreness and irritation in the nose and throat as well as breathing problems like asthma.

Smog hangs over the city of Los Angeles, USA.

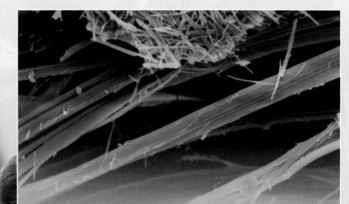

Allergies and lung problems

Breathing problems lower down in the breathing system may be caused by problems with the organs themselves, or by an overly protective reaction by the body, which is known as an allergy.

It's Amazing!

A single person sheds about 1.5 grams of skin cells every day. That is enough to feed up to a million dust mites.

Too protective?

Allergic reactions are the body's response to allergens, or foreign substances – even though these substances might be harmless. When the body detects an allergen it triggers the release of chemicals, which start a sequence of reactions designed to protect the body. Some of these reactions, however, such as a runny nose and sneezing, can be a nuisance – while others can be dangerous.

Hay fever

Hay fever is an allergic response that is triggered by tiny pollen grains. These grains are produced by plants in spring and summer. When the pollen grains are breathed in, they cause the body to release a chemical called histamine. This chemical irritates the linings of the breathing system, causing a runny nose and sneezing.

A microscopic view of pollen grains

Top Facts

- Some allergic reactions are treated using drugs called antihistamines. These stop the production of histamine.

- The name 'asthma' comes from the Greek word meaning 'sharp breath'.

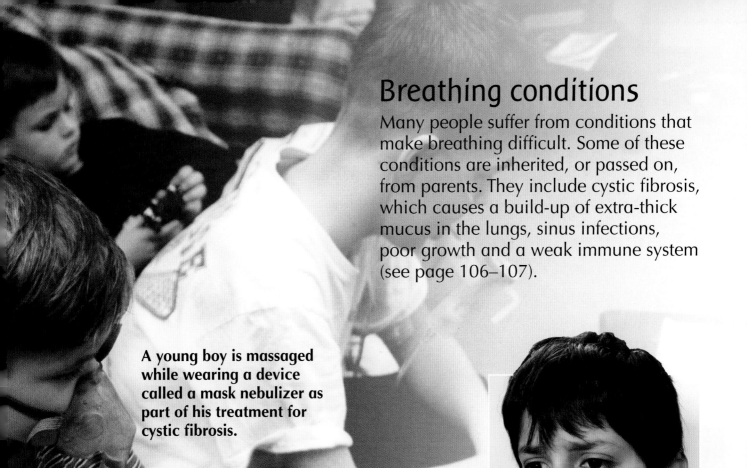

Breathing conditions

Many people suffer from conditions that make breathing difficult. Some of these conditions are inherited, or passed on, from parents. They include cystic fibrosis, which causes a build-up of extra-thick mucus in the lungs, sinus infections, poor growth and a weak immune system (see page 106–107).

A young boy is massaged while wearing a device called a mask nebulizer as part of his treatment for cystic fibrosis.

A boy uses an inhaler to treat asthma.

Tiny creatures

Dust mites are tiny creatures that feed on the dust found in our homes and work places. The waste products they leave behind are a major cause of allergic responses in many people, such as asthma (see right).

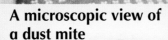

A microscopic view of a dust mite

Asthma

Asthma is a condition that inflames the breathing passages, causing them to constrict, or narrow, so much that breathing becomes difficult. Asthma can be caused by many things, including allergens, cold air, exercise or stress.

Keeping airways and lungs healthy

Keeping the airways clear and healthy is vital for our well-being. Getting oxygen into our bodies is essential, and any reduction in the amount of this gas could have disastrous consequences.

A cyclist wears a mask to reduce the amount of traffic fumes he inhales.

Deep breath

As with any muscles, the intercostal muscles and the diaphragm (see pages 76–77) benefit from regular exercise. This helps to make them stronger and to improve your breathing system.

A cloud of water droplets breathed out by a walker on a cold day.

Moisture in breath

The air you breathe out contains more water vapour than the air you breathe in – you can see a cloud of water vapour when you breathe out on a cold day. This highlights one of the ways in which the body loses water (see page 133). It is important that we do not lose too much water. We need to drink plenty of liquids throughout the day.

It's Amazing!

The average person breathes about 21,600 times every day. This draws about 8000 litres of air into the lungs every 24 hours.

Keeping fit

Exercise is important for keeping the breathing system healthy. Long periods of exercise, called cardiovascular exercise, include walking, running, cycling and swimming. This type of exercise gets you breathing harder than normal, which exercises the muscles involved in breathing and makes them stronger.

Going for a long walk or run can improve your breathing system.

Water in breath

- Place a small mirror in the fridge for an hour.
- Take the mirror out and then breathe out over it.
- You will see that the mirror fogs up where you breathe on it. This fog on the mirror is caused by the water vapour in the air you breathe out.

Keeping bad stuff out

Every day, you breathe in substances that are bad for your body. Most of the time, your body can get rid of these using a variety of actions, such as coughing and sneezing. Exposure to excessive amounts of bad chemicals, however, such as cigarette smoke and traffic fumes, can have dangerous effects, including lung diseases and cancer.

Even if you don't smoke, breathing in another person's cigarette smoke can be dangerous.

Smoking

Smoking is bad for the breathing system. The smoke strips away the cilia from the linings of the airways, making it hard to remove excess mucus and potentially dangerous substances. The smoke also contains more than 4000 chemicals, some 69 of which are known to cause cancer.

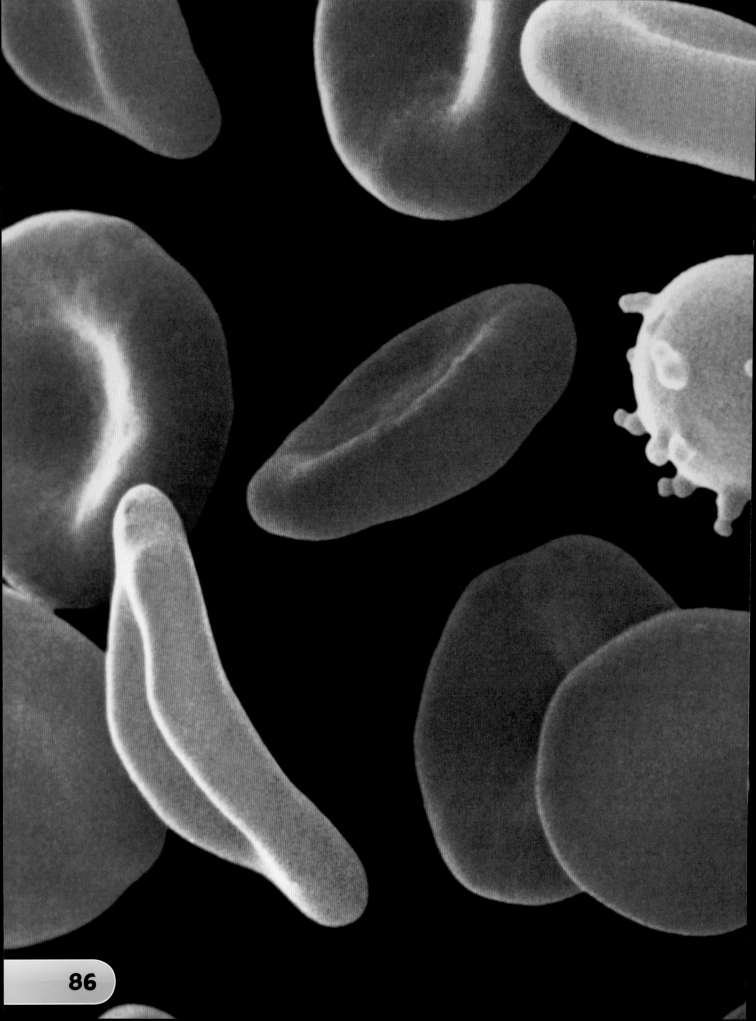

HEART AND BLOOD

The heart is an amazing pump that works non-stop, keeping the body alive. With every beat, it sends a surge of bright-red blood, carrying vital supplies, such as oxygen, and the body's waste products, such as carbon dioxide, through a network of blood vessels to and from every part of the body. The heart, blood and vessels are together known as the circulatory, or cardiovascular, system.

Non-stop pump

The heart is a muscular pump that works constantly to squeeze blood into blood vessels called arteries. The arteries take the blood around the body, and the veins return the blood to the heart.

The mechanical pump of a fountain uses force to squirt water a great distance.

Powerful pump

Just like a fountain forces water out, the heart muscle contracts to push blood at great force into the arteries. Your heart will do this about two-and-a-half billion times during your life.

The right pump

The heart is really two pumps side by side. The right pump sends blood along the pulmonary arteries to the lungs, where it absorbs oxygen. This blood then comes back along the pulmonary veins to the left side of the heart to be pumped around the rest of the body (see right).

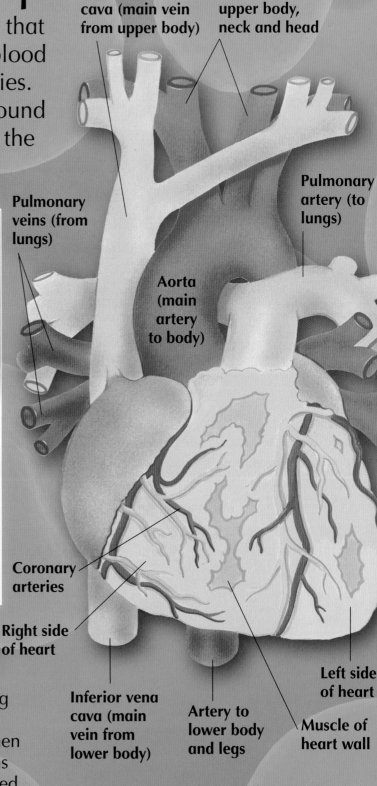

Superior vena cava (main vein from upper body)

Arteries to upper body, neck and head

Pulmonary veins (from lungs)

Pulmonary artery (to lungs)

Aorta (main artery to body)

Coronary arteries

Right side of heart

Inferior vena cava (main vein from lower body)

Artery to lower body and legs

Left side of heart

Muscle of heart wall

A view of the outside of the heart and main blood vessels

Valves stop blood from flowing the wrong way in the veins.

Valves

Normal direction of blood flow

Studying veins

The veins are just under the skin in some places, and can be seen as dark lines. The blood in the veins does not flow with as much pressure as the blood being forced through the arteries by the heart. Because vein blood flows with a lower pressure, there is a risk that it could flow the wrong way. To stop this, the larger veins have valves in them, and these slam shut to stop blood from flowing the wrong way.

It's Amazing!

With each pump, blood surges out into the main arteries at a speed of 40 centimetres per second. If it were to pass through a hole the size of a pinhead at this speed and pressure, it would spurt more than 3 metres.

The left pump

The left side of the heart is larger and more powerful than the right side. While the right side of the heart pumps blood to the lungs, the left side pumps blood all around the body, delivering oxygen, energy and nutrients from food to every part. Then the blood, which is now low in oxygen, returns from all of these body parts along the veins to the heart's right side. There, it begins its non-stop journey back to the lungs and then around the body once again.

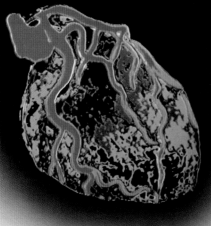

An image of the heart with the coronary arteries shown in red.

Blood supply

The heart muscle has its own blood supply – the coronary arteries. Blood flows along these arteries into the heart muscle and then out along the coronary veins. If the coronary arteries become blocked, the heart muscle may die. This is one form of a heart attack.

Harvey's discovery

For centuries, people believed that blood flowed into the body, where it was used up. In 1628, English physician William Harvey did experiments that showed that blood circulates around and around the body in the blood vessels, returning to the heart at the end of each circuit.

Inside the heart

The heart is not a solid lump of muscle but has four inner compartments, called chambers. Blood flows through these chambers, with four valves, or flaps, making sure that it flows the right way.

Upper chambers

Each half of the heart has an upper chamber, which is called an atrium. The left atrium receives blood from the lungs. The right atrium takes in blood from the body.

The blue arrows show the passage of blood from the body into the right side of the heart. The red arrows show the passage of blood from the lungs through the left side of the heart.

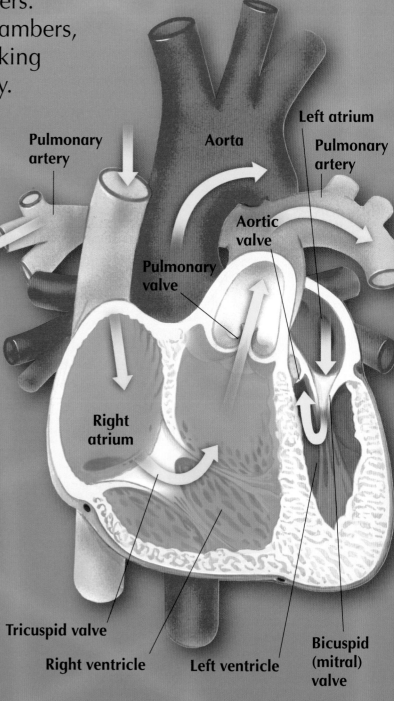

Pulmonary artery

Aorta

Left atrium

Pulmonary artery

Aortic valve

Pulmonary valve

Right atrium

Tricuspid valve

Right ventricle

Left ventricle

Bicuspid (mitral) valve

A cutaway view of the heart showing the four chambers and the valves inside.

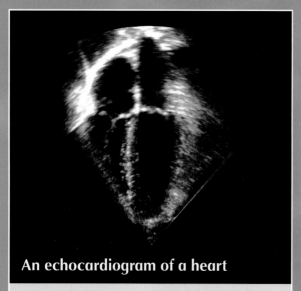

An echocardiogram of a heart

Echocardiogram

Sound waves can be beamed into the heart, where they hit different parts and echo back. These echoes form a moving picture called an echocardiogram, which shows the four chambers of the heart.

Lower chambers

Each side of the heart also has a lower chamber, which is called a ventricle. Each ventricle receives blood from the atrium above it through a funnel-shaped valve. As the ventricles squeeze, they push blood out through one-way valves into the main arteries.

Top Facts

- In a typical adult at rest, the heart pumps about 70 times each minute and sends out about 70 millilitres of blood with each beat.

- The heart pumps about 5 litres of blood each minute, which is the total volume of blood in an adult body. When the heart pumps faster, it sends out four times this amount.

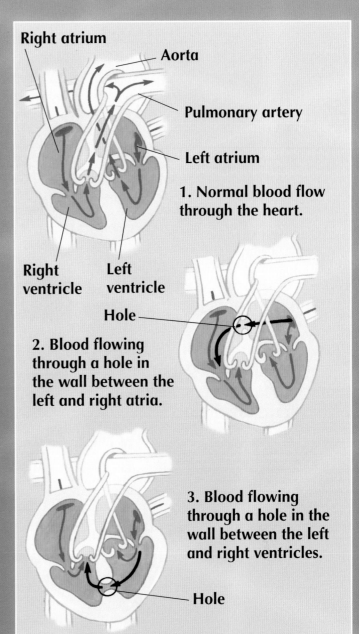

Right atrium

Aorta

Pulmonary artery

Left atrium

Right ventricle

Left ventricle

1. Normal blood flow through the heart.

Hole

2. Blood flowing through a hole in the wall between the left and right atria.

3. Blood flowing through a hole in the wall between the left and right ventricles.

Hole

Hole in the heart

Some babies are born with a heart problem called a 'hole in the heart'. With this condition, blood from one side of the heart can mix with blood from the other side. As a result, not enough oxygen and nutrients reach the body's cells, resulting in shortness of breath, tiredness, heart failure and even a stroke. Sometimes, these holes close naturally, but an operation may be needed.

How the heart beats

A heartbeat is a sequence of actions that makes blood flow through the heart's chambers and valves, into the body and back to the heart again.

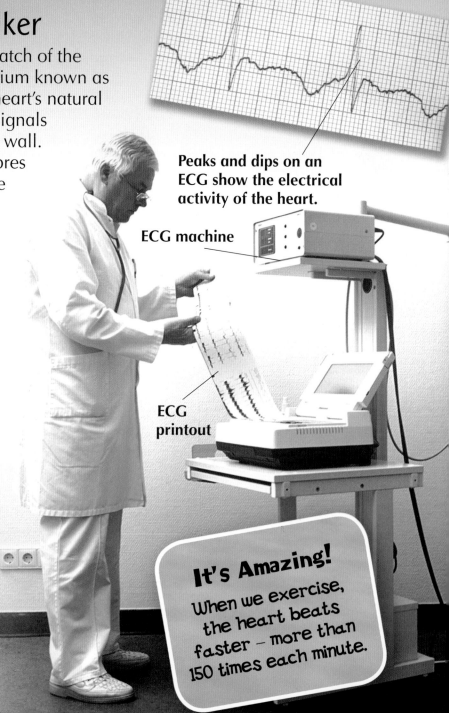

A doctor checks an ECG reading in order to monitor the effect of exercise on a man's heart.

The natural pacemaker

A heartbeat begins in a small patch of the heart wall in the upper right atrium known as the sinoatrial node. This is the heart's natural pacemaker, sending electrical signals through the muscle of the heart wall. The signals make the muscle fibres of the heart shorten, causing the whole heart to contract.

Peaks and dips on an ECG show the electrical activity of the heart.

ECG machine

ECG printout

The pulse can be felt by placing the fingers on the wrist above the thumb.

The pulse

As blood leaves the heart with each beat, it surges into the arteries and makes them pulsate, or bulge. This pulsation is called the pulse. The veins do not pulsate because the blood pressure inside them is too low.

It's Amazing!

When we exercise, the heart beats faster – more than 150 times each minute.

A heartbeat

The 'lub-dub' sound of the heartbeat is made by the valves in the heart slapping shut. With every single heartbeat, the heart muscles contract to pump blood around the body. They then relax and more blood flows into the heart from the veins.

1. As a heartbeat starts, blood passes at low pressure from the main veins into the atria.

2. The atria contract to push the blood through the valves into the ventricles.

3. The ventricle walls contract to put great pressure on the blood inside.

4. The blood surges out through valves into the main arteries.

Sensors

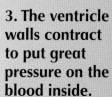

Under control

The natural pacemaker has its own steady rhythm – usually about 70 beats a minute – but the rhythm can be altered, depending on what the body needs. Nerves bring electrical messages from the cardiac centre in the lower brain that make the pacemaker speed up or slow down its rhythm. The messenger hormone called adrenaline (see pages 158–159), also affects the speed and power of the heartbeat.

Pacemaker

Sometimes the heart does not beat regularly. This is known as cardiac arrhythmia. It may beat too fast (tachycardia), too slow (bradycardia) or tremble in a chaotic way (fibrillate). An artificial electronic pacemaker can be fitted to the heart to make the rhythm regular again.

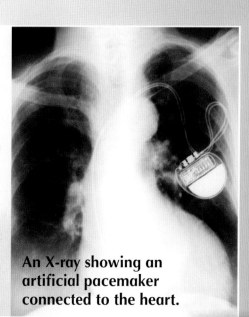

An X-ray showing an artificial pacemaker connected to the heart.

Around and around

The blood circulates, or flows, around the body in a system of blood vessels called the vascular network. Arteries take blood away from the heart, veins bring it back again and tiny vessels called capillaries connect the arteries and veins.

Two systems

Just as the heart is two pumps, the circulation has two parts. The arteries and veins that lead to and from the left side of the heart are known as the systemic circulation. The systemic arteries deliver oxygen, energy, nutrients and other important substances to the body's billions of microscopic cells. The systemic veins then collect waste products.

To the brain

Blood flows to the brain up the carotid artery in the neck. This artery's pulse can be felt as blood surges through it with each heartbeat. In an emergency, medical staff check the carotid pulse to make sure that the brain is receiving enough blood.

A doctor feels the carotid pulse in this man's neck.

Jugular vein

Carotid artery

Aorta (main artery)

Superior vena cava

Heart

Radial artery

Lower aorta (main artery)

Inferior vena cava (main vein from body)

Iliac vein

Iliac artery

The main blood vessels of the circulation. Arteries are shown in red and veins in blue. Capillaries are too small to see in this diagram.

Lungs and oxygen

The second set of arteries and veins takes blood from the right side of the heart to the lungs for more oxygen. This system is called the pulmonary circulation. As the blood leaves the heart, it is low in oxygen and dark reddish-blue. In the lungs, the blood absorbs oxygen, turns bright red and flows back to the left side of the heart.

Tibial vein

Tibial artery

Top Facts

- It takes a drop of blood one minute to travel around the entire systemic circulation.

- The time taken for one drop to pass around the pulmonary circulation is less than 10 seconds.

- In the systemic circulation, arteries carry bright red, oxygen-rich blood.

- In the pulmonary circulation, the arteries carry dark reddish-blue blood that is low in oxygen.

It's Amazing!

If all your blood vessels could be taken out of your body and laid end to end, they would stretch 100,000 kilometres. This is the same distance as two-and-a-half times around the Earth!

After exercise, we have to stop to allow our bodies to recover.

Exhausted

During exercise, the muscles need more oxygen and energy, so the heart beats faster to supply more blood. After exercising for a while, the circulation cannot keep up. We have to slow down and breathe faster and deeper to take in more oxygen, which allows the circulation to settle down again.

Blood cells

An adult has about 5 litres of blood in his or her body. This thick, red, sticky fluid is essential to life – without it we would die. It does many vital jobs, including carrying oxygen around the body, removing waste and fighting disease.

Red blood cells

Blood consists of billions of microscopic cells floating in a liquid called plasma. There are three main kinds of cells – the most numerous are red blood cells, also known as erythrocytes. They are shaped like doughnuts without the holes, and their main task is to take in oxygen from the lungs and release it to the organs and tissues.

A magnified image of red blood cells

It's Amazing!

A tiny drop of blood as small as a pinhead contains approximately 5 million red blood cells, 10,000 white blood cells and 300,000 platelets.

Plasma: 55% ——————

White blood cells and platelets: 4% ——

Red blood cells: 41% ——————

What's in blood?

More than half of blood is liquid plasma, which is mostly water. Plasma also contains nutrients, glucose, hormones and hundreds of other substances. The red and white cells and the platelets (see page 97) move about in the liquid plasma.

Other blood cells

The second kind of blood cells are white blood cells, known as leucocytes (see pages 106–107). These cells fight germs and disease and remove waste from the blood and body. The third kind of cells are platelets (see pages 102–103), also called thrombocytes. These are more like cell fragments, and their major task is to help blood clot in cuts and wounds to form a scab.

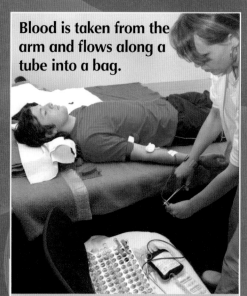

Blood is taken from the arm and flows along a tube into a bag.

Giving blood

Many people donate, or give, blood. The body makes up the lost blood in a few days. Giving blood saves millions of lives around the world every year.

Blood groups

In 1901, Austrian doctor Karl Landsteiner realized that not all blood is the same. Different people have blood from different groups. These groups are labelled A, B, AB and O. If blood of the wrong group is given to a person, it can kill them.

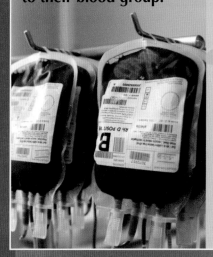

Bags of donated blood are labelled according to their blood group.

Storing blood

Donated blood is tested for infections and to find out its blood group. It is then stored in a blood bank, ready to be used if someone needs it during an operation or because of an accident. The blood is transfused, or passed, into the patient through a tube connected to a vein.

Blood vessels

When blood leaves the heart, it passes through strong, thick-walled arteries. These split and branch many times to form tiny capillaries (see pages 100–101), which then join to the veins that carry the blood back to the heart.

To the heart

The blood flowing through the veins is under low pressure. As veins approach the heart, they get wider and wider until they pour into two very large veins. These are the superior vena cava, which brings blood from the head and arms, and the inferior vena cava, which brings blood from the legs and trunk (see pages 94–95).

Varicose veins

Varicose veins are veins that appear as twisted lumps under the skin. They are caused by the vein walls becoming weak and the veins widening. This means that the valves cannot work properly and they allow blood to flow the wrong way. Compare this with the diagram of a properly working vein on page 89. As the blood flows the wrong way, it makes the veins bulge and forms bumps on the skin.

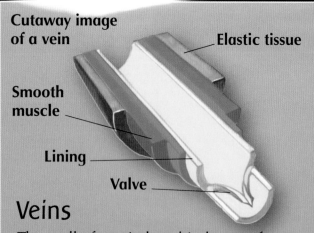

Cutaway image of a vein

Elastic tissue

Smooth muscle

Lining

Valve

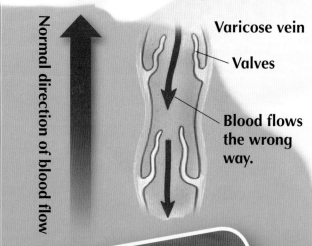

Normal direction of blood flow

Varicose vein

Valves

Blood flows the wrong way.

Veins

The wall of a vein has thin layers of smooth muscle. These muscles contract to keep the blood moving towards the heart. In many of the larger veins, the inner lining has flaps that act as valves, which stop the blood from going the wrong way.

It's Amazing!

At any moment, more than 70 per cent of the blood is in the veins, about 20 per cent is in the arteries and less than 10 per cent is in the smallest blood vessels, the capillaries.

Looking at blood vessels

- Have a look at the inside of your wrist. You can probably see blue lines under the skin.
- These are veins carrying blood from the hands. You can't usually see the arteries in the wrist because they are deeper under the skin and have thicker walls that hide the blood.

Taking blood from a vein in the arm using a hollow needle.

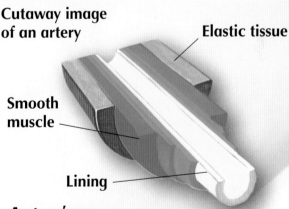

Cutaway image of an artery

Elastic tissue

Smooth muscle

Lining

From the heart

Blood is pumped from the heart under great pressure. Arteries have thicker walls than veins to withstand this high blood pressure without bursting. They also have layers of muscles in their walls that can tighten to make the artery narrower. The brain controls the width of the arteries, allowing it to alter the amount of blood that flows to each body part.

Arteries

An artery's wall has several layers – the inner layer is a smooth lining along which blood flows, the middle layer is muscle and the outer layer is elastic tissue. The muscles contract to squeeze the artery, pushing the blood along.

Smallest blood vessels

The tiniest blood vessels, the capillaries, are far too thin to see except through a microscope. They form a fine mesh that carries important nutrients to almost every cell within your body and takes away potentially harmful waste products.

Capillary network

Capillaries form as arteries branch again and again, becoming narrower and shorter. Almost every part of the body has a network of capillaries branching among its cells and tissues. Only a few parts, such as the lens of the eye, lack capillaries. The smallest capillaries are in the brain and intestine, and the largest are in the bone marrow and skin.

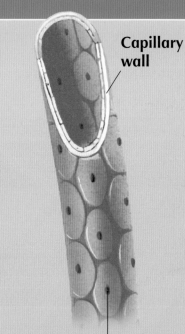

Capillary wall

Endothelial cell

Cutaway view of a capillary

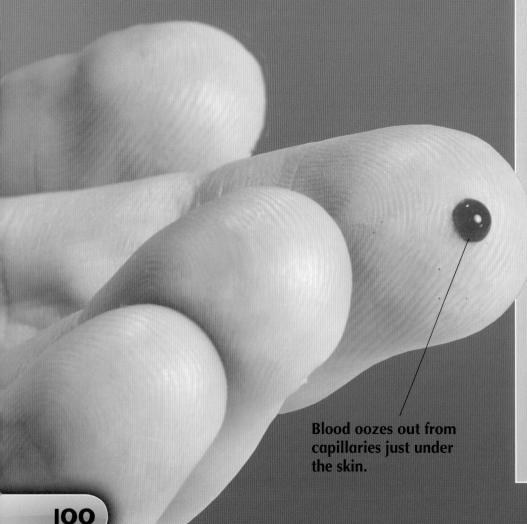

Blood oozes out from capillaries just under the skin.

Thin walls

The wall of a capillary is made of a single layer of endothelial cells. The walls are so thin that most substances can pass through them. Red blood cells cannot pass, but white cells can squeeze through to attack germs.

Tight squeeze

The smallest capillaries are not much wider than a red blood cell – if they were laid side by side, you could fit about 70 red blood cells across the full stop at the end of this sentence. The red blood cells have to line up in single file to pass through the narrowest capillaries.

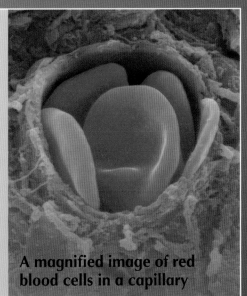

A magnified image of red blood cells in a capillary

Waste and heat

In the lungs, oxygen passes through the network of capillaries into the blood, and the waste gas carbon dioxide goes the other way. Other waste products pass from the blood through capillaries into the kidneys and intestines, where they are removed from the body. The body also removes excess heat through the capillaries. The heat passes from the blood through capillaries into the skin, where it is released.

Top Facts

- An average capillary is 0.01 millimetres wide and it is 0.1 millimetres long.

- A typical artery is 10 millimetres wide and 15 centimetres in length.

- An average vein is 10 millimetres wide and measures about 20 centimetres long.

- The widest artery, the aorta, measures 25 millimetres across.

- The largest veins, the venae cavae, are 30 millimetres across.

It's Amazing!

There are more than 10 billion capillaries running through nearly every part of the body. If they were all laid out flat, they would cover 5000 square metres, which is almost the area of a football pitch.

Blood pressure

Blood presses on the walls of the blood vessels as it flows through them. This force is called blood pressure and is measured using a machine called a sphygmomanometer. Two readings are usually taken – the higher systolic pressure when the heart pumps out blood and the lower diastolic pressure when the heart relaxes.

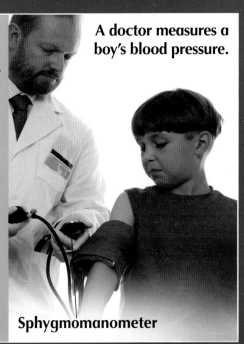

A doctor measures a boy's blood pressure.

Sphygmomanometer

Blood clotting

One of blood's vital tasks is to seal wounds by forming a clot. If blood didn't form clots, people would bleed to death from small cuts.

Internal clots

As well as forming to heal a cut on the surface of the skin (see pages 20–21), blood clots form to block leaks that occur inside the body. In fact, tiny leaks are forming inside your body all the time. If your blood wasn't able to clot, then you would die from internal bleeding.

Platelets clump together.

Platelets grow spines and bind to each other.

Platelet plugs

Within a few seconds of a blood vessel being damaged, platelets in the blood collect near the injury. They swell, become sticky and clump together to form a plug that stops blood flowing from the wound. The plug creates a surface on which the clot can form.

Clotting experiment

- Pour water through a sieve. It should flow through easily. Place a sheet of kitchen paper into the sieve and slowly pour on water.
- The fibres in the paper will swell and slow the passage of water like the fibres in a blood clot.

Travelling clots

An embolus is an object in the bloodstream that may block a blood vessel, especially where the vessel divides into smaller branches. A blood clot that forms in one part of the vessel network, such as a vein, may travel in the blood. It could block a coronary artery in the heart, causing a heart attack, or an artery in the brain, leading to a stroke.

An open wound during surgery. The wound is not bleeding heavily because the blood has clotted.

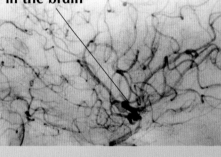

An embolism in an artery in the brain

Embolisms

Sometimes, a thrombus, or clot, forms where a blood vessel is narrowed due to a build-up of fatty patches, called atheroma, in its lining. The clot may then detach to become an embolus and travel through the body.

Leeches

Leeches feed on blood, and there is a substance in their saliva that stops blood from clotting. Some surgeons use leeches today because they stop blood clotting in wounds. This keeps blood flowing to damaged body parts and speeds up recovery.

Common leech

It's Amazing!

The blood clotting process is extremely complicated and can involve more than 30 different chemicals.

The lymph system

A fluid called lymph travels around the body in tubes similar to blood vessels. These lymphatics, or lymph vessels, have small masses of tissue along them called lymph nodes.

Lymph fluid

Lymph is a pale, clear fluid that collects between cells and tissues. It flows into lymph vessels and ends up in larger vessels called lymphatic ducts. These empty the lymph into the blood system.

One-way flow

Unlike the circulatory system, the lymph system does not flow in a cycle. Instead, it starts with tiny, dead-end capillaries, which form a network of tubes that weave between tissue cells. The walls of the capillaries are just one cell thick. Fluid from the tissue moves into the capillaries through openings between the cells in the lymph capillary wall.

Tissue cell

Endothelial cell (lymph capillary lining)

Lymph

Fluid from tissue enters lymph

Opening in capillary

Ending of lymph capillary

Tonsils

Cervical (neck) nodes

Thymus gland

Spleen

Lumbar nodes

Thoracic duct

Intestinal nodes

Inguinal nodes

Iliac nodes

What lymph does

Like blood, lymph delivers nutrients and takes away waste. It also carries white blood cells that fight germs and disease (see pages 106–107). The lymph nodes are packed with white blood cells, which clean the lymph and kill germs. There is no pump like the heart to push lymph around the body. Instead, it flows slowly, squeezed by muscles around the lymph vessels. Lymph only moves when the body's muscles are active.

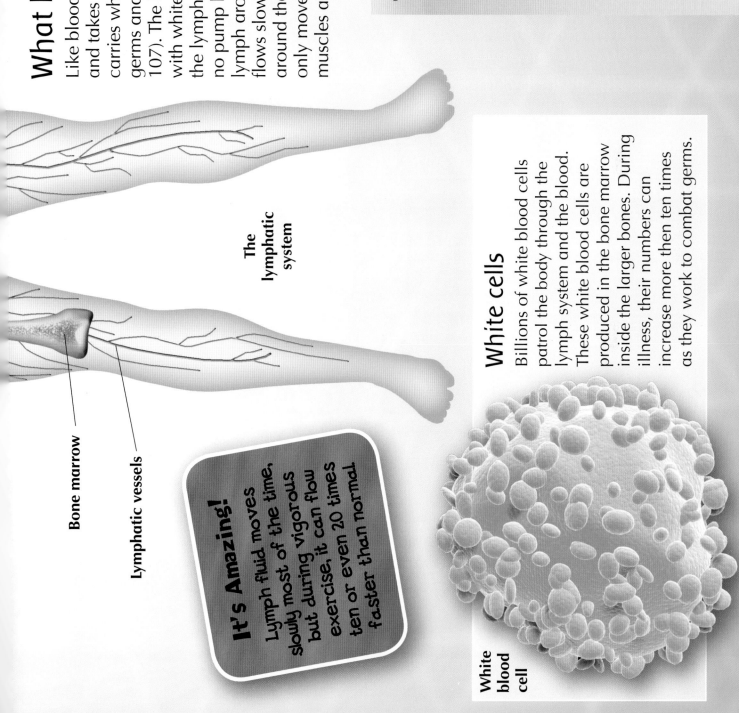

Bone marrow

Lymphatic vessels

The lymphatic system

It's Amazing!
Lymph fluid moves slowly most of the time, but during vigorous exercise, it can flow ten or even 20 times faster than normal.

Top Facts

- The average adult body contains between 1 and 2 litres of lymph fluid.

- Each lymph node is between 1 and 25 millimetres wide.

- Nodes get their name from a Latin word that means 'knot' because the rows of nodes resemble knots in a piece of string.

White cells

Billions of white blood cells patrol the body through the lymph system and the blood. These white blood cells are produced in the bone marrow inside the larger bones. During illness, their numbers can increase more then ten times as they work to combat germs.

White blood cell

Fighting disease

If a germ enters your body, it can make you unwell. Your body has a mini army of different white blood cells, such as lymphocytes, neutrophils and macrophages, and organs, such as the spleen, that are always ready to fight germs. These make up your body's immune system.

First line of attack

Any germs that enter the body are attacked by white blood cells called macrophages. Each macrophage surrounds a germ and carries it in the lymph to a lymph node. There, other white blood cells called lymphocytes get to work.

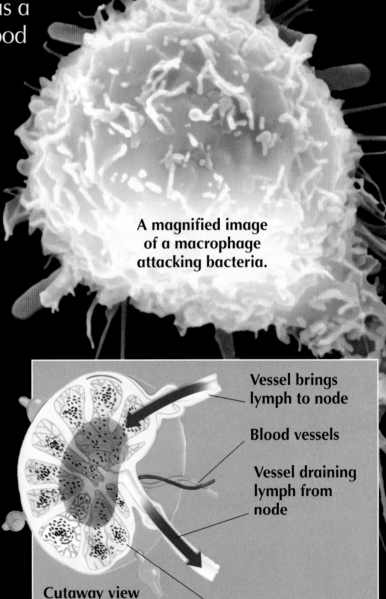

A magnified image of a macrophage attacking bacteria.

Vessel brings lymph to node

Blood vessels

Vessel draining lymph from node

Cutaway view of a lymph node

Lymph nodule

White globules

White blood cells were first identified through a microscope in the 18th century. The role of these white cells was not understood at the time, and they were called 'white globules of pus'.

Lymph nodes

White blood cells called lymphocytes multiply and are stored inside the lymph nodes. Lymph flows into the node, bringing germs and other harmful substances to these concentrations of white blood cells.

Germ destroyers

Macrophages can destroy things that the body doesn't recognize as belonging to it, including bacteria. They do this by surrounding the invader and digesting it in a process called phagocytosis.

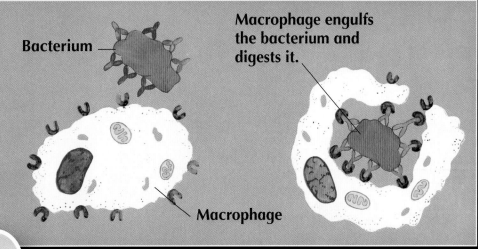

Bacterium

Macrophage engulfs the bacterium and digests it.

Macrophage

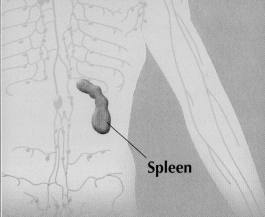

Spleen

Spleen

The spleen is an organ that filters waste substances from the blood and lymph. It also acts as a large store for red and white blood cells, in case the body should loose a lot of blood suddenly.

Lymphocytes

T lymphocytes identify germs by recognizing foreign substances on their surfaces called antigens. B lymphocytes then produce substances called antibodies that find other germs of this type and stick to them. Macrophages then destroy the germs and antibodies. Some antibodies remain in the body, so that it can respond quickly to a germ if it invades again.

Heart and blood problems

The heart and blood play such a vital role in keeping the body alive that any problems with them can be serious. If a problem is found, however, there are many modern treatments that can help.

Fainting

Sometimes, the heart cannot pump enough blood up to the brain. This may happen if a person has to stand for a long time, especially in hot weather. The body's reaction is to faint – lose consciousness and fall over. Fainting brings the heart level with the head, so it can pump blood to the brain more easily.

This doctor is listening to a boy's heart though a stethoscope.

Hearing the heart

Doctors listen to the sounds of a heartbeat to make sure the heart is working properly. Unusual sounds known as murmurs may indicate that the blood is not flowing normally.

Standing for a long time has made this soldier faint.

Heart attack

A heart attack happens when the blood flow to the heart is interrupted, which may be because of a blood clot (see pages 102–103) blocking an artery. Without oxygen or energy, the heart muscle cannot beat properly. This causes chest pain, breathlessness, sweating and feeling faint. If the blood flow to the heart is not restored within about 40 minutes, the heart muscle will begin to die.

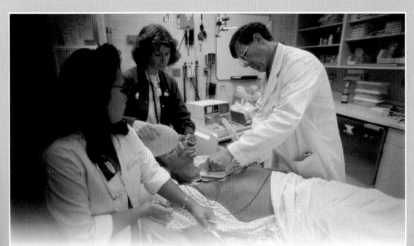

Medical staff use a defibrillator in an emergency.

Shocking the heart

A heart that is not beating properly can be shocked into a regular rhythm by using an electrical charge. This is passed into the heart via two pads on the chest from a machine called a defibrillator.

Bad blood

Until the end of the 19th century, many doctors treated a wide variety of illnesses by blood-letting. This involved cutting a patient in the belief that removing the 'bad blood' would stop an illness from getting worse.

It's Amazing!

With modern emergency treatments, such as defibrillators, the chances of surviving a heart attack are twice what they were 50 years ago.

Too narrow

Over many years, a diet that is too high in fats (see pages 116–117) can lead to a fatty substance building up in the lining of the arteries. This condition, called atherosclerosis, makes the arteries narrow and harden, decreasing the flow of blood and making it more likely that a clot will form.

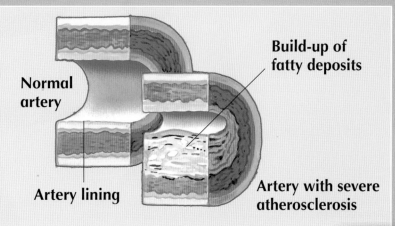

Build-up of fatty deposits

Normal artery

Artery lining

Artery with severe atherosclerosis

Healthy heart and blood

All muscles need exercise or they will become weak and waste away. The heart is almost all muscle, and, like all muscles it gets stronger if it is exercised on a regular basis.

Daily exercise

Exercise keeps the lungs, bones, joints and many other body parts healthy, but it doesn't have to involve playing sport or working out in the gym. Exercise can be a part of daily life, such as walking or cycling rather than sitting in a car, or using the stairs rather than lifts or escalators.

It's Amazing!

An average person's heart pumps more than 100,000 times a day and 40 million times a year. Over a lifetime, this adds up to around three billion beats.

Playing a sport, such as football, is a great way to get the heart pumping fast.

Top Facts

To keep your circulatory system healthy you should:

- Exercise regularly – at least two or three times a week for at least 20 minutes.

- Eat a balanced diet, low in fats, salt and processed foods.

- Keep your weight at a healthy level.

- Not smoke.

- Try to reduce worry, stress and anxiety.

Quit it!

Apart from damaging the lungs, smoking makes it more likely that blood vessels will narrow. It also reduces the ability of the blood to carry oxygen.

Smoking increases the risk of heart disease.

Importance of diet

What we eat also has a great effect on the heart and blood. Eating foods that contains a lot of the mineral iron (see below) helps to keep our red blood cells healthy. On the other hand, eating too much salt can cause blood pressure to rise and put extra strain on the heart and blood vessels.

Iron-rich food	Iron Content per 100 g	RDA %
Cockles boiled	28 mg	155%
Liver	9 mg	50%
Fish paste	9 mg	50%
Kidney	8 mg	44%
Venison	7.8 mg	43%
Mussels boiled	7 mg	39%
Liver pâté	7 mg	39%
Liver sausage	6.4 mg	36%
Goose	5 mg	28%
Shrimps	5 mg	28%
Sardines	4.5 mg	27%
Anchovies	4 mg	22%
Whitebait	4 mg	22%
Lean beef	2.5 mg	16%

A list of foods with high levels of iron. The RDA is the amount of a nutrient experts recommend a person should eat each day.

Eat well

Eating a balanced diet helps to keep the digestive system working well and contains all the vitamins and minerals needed to keep the blood healthy.

A salad containing a lot of vegetables is a healthy choice of meal.

FOOD AND DIGESTION

Why do we need food? It gives us energy for our muscles as we move about, and it also provides energy for all the processes that happen inside our bodies. Food supplies the raw materials needed for growth in babies and children and to mend everyday wear and tear. Food is also tasty and a pleasure to eat. The parts of the body that deal with food – from the first bite to getting rid of the waste – are known as the digestive system.

Food's journey

Swallowing is the start of a long journey for your food that takes 24 hours or more and involves travelling up to 9 metres through a dark tube full of powerful chemicals.

Digestive tract

The digestive tract is a long tube that starts at the mouth and ends at the anus. Food is chewed in the mouth, swallowed down the throat and pushed through the oesophagus, or gullet, into the stomach. It then travels through the small and large intestines to the anus, where any waste is passed out.

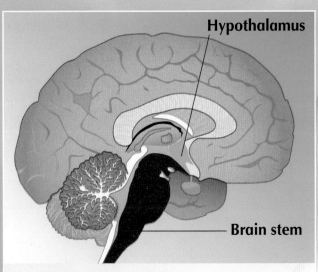

Hypothalamus

Brain stem

Thinking of food

The brain plays a vital role in digestion. A part called the hypothalamus makes us feel hungry and thirsty. The brain stem lies between the spinal cord and the upper brain. It controls the automatic movements of the gut and the removal of food waste.

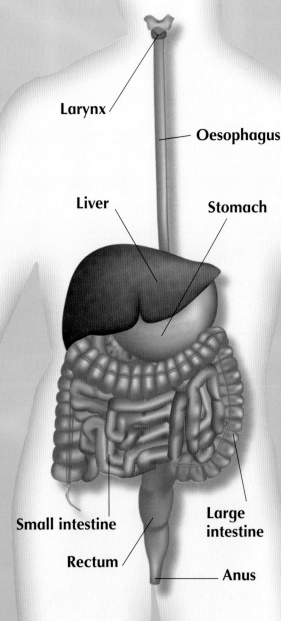

Larynx

Oesophagus

Liver

Stomach

Small intestine

Large intestine

Rectum

Anus

Most of the digestive system is packed into the lower half of the body – the abdomen.

Food study

In 1822, American doctor William Beaumont attended a patient who had been shot in the stomach. The small bullet hole was kept open and provided a 'window' for studying what happened in the stomach. Beaumont poked into the hole and took samples of the chemicals that the stomach made after the patient ate.

Breaking down food

In the digestive tract, the food is digested, or broken down, and absorbed into the body. Anything that isn't absorbed or used by the body is expelled as waste. Several other body parts help with the digestion of food, including the liver and pancreas. They create some of the chemicals needed to break down and absorb food.

Plenty of water

As well as food, the body also needs water. Water is essential for almost every process in the body – from digestion to sweating. Some water is contained in food, but everyone should also drink plenty of water.

The body needs water to survive.

Big eater

Elephants have huge bodies, which need a lot of energy. They eat mainly grass, leaves and other plant foods that are low in nourishment. So to get enough energy from its diet, an adult elephant must eat for about 18 to 20 hours every day. An elephant can eat more than 200 kilograms of plant food daily, which is about the weight of three adult humans.

An elephant grasps food with its trunk and chews with its huge teeth.

It's Amazing!

In a year, an adult human needs to eat more than half a tonne of food. That's half the weight of a small car. An adult also needs to drink about 700 litres of water, which is enough to fill 50 baths.

What's in food?

Food is not just needed to fill us up and ward off hunger. It contains hundreds of substances that your body must have to stay fit and healthy and to work well.

The right balance

The body needs the right balance of different types of food. Too much of any single food item can cause harm. A healthy balance contains plenty of fruit and vegetables, grains, such as bread, pasta and rice, some fish and dairy produce and not too much meat, especially red meat. Foods that are high in sugar and fats should only be eaten in small quantities.

This food pyramid shows how much of each type of food you should eat in a healthy diet.

Fats

Sugar

Dairy, meat, fish and eggs

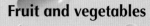

Fruit and vegetables

Grains: bread, pasta, rice and cereal

It's Amazing!

Every few weeks, a new fad diet comes and goes. But the basics of healthy eating have been the same since people lived in caves!

Food for energy

Different foods contain a variety of substances, and they all perform different roles once they have been absorbed by the body. For example, vitamins and minerals help to keep the body working well. Proteins are important for building new cells and tissue, as well as repairing damaged ones. Carbohydrates are used to supply the energy we need to live.

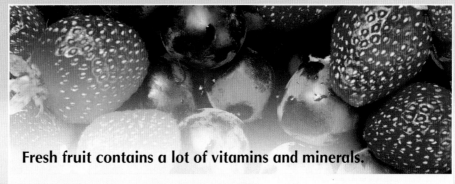

Fresh fruit contains a lot of vitamins and minerals.

Vitamins and minerals

There are many vitamins and minerals that are important to your body. For example, vitamin C helps to keep your gums healthy, while vitamin D helps to keep your bones strong. The mineral iron is important for healthy blood.

Protein

Meat and fish contain a lot of protein.

Meat, fish, eggs, nuts, pulses and cheese contain a lot of protein. Your body breaks down the protein you eat into simpler chemicals called amino acids. It can then use these amino acids to build new proteins to make and repair body cells.

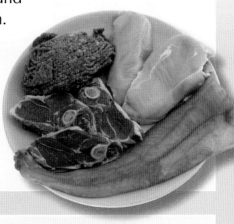

Carbohydrates

Sugar and starch are foods that contain a lot of carbohydrates. While your body needs these substances to make energy, if you eat too many carbohydrates, your body turns them into fat. It then stores this fat in a layer just under the skin called the adipose tissue.

Bread contains a lot of carbohydrates.

Top Facts

- An important part of food, which the body does not digest, is fibre. Fibre helps the intestines to stay healthy. Fruit and vegetables and wholemeal foods – in which every part of the grain is used – contain a lot of fibre.

- Processed foods have been changed so much that they lose some of their natural goodness. White bread, for example, has very little fibre left.

Teeth and biting

Teeth bite, grind and chew food to make it easier to swallow and digest. They are coated with enamel – the hardest material in the body – so that they last a long time. In fact, you will only have two sets of teeth throughout your entire lifetime!

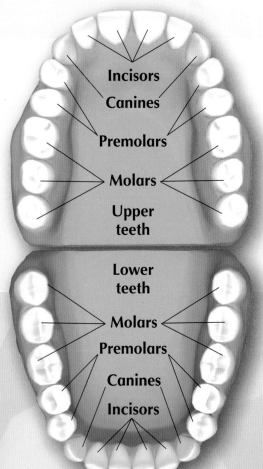

The full set

An adult has 32 teeth. There are four different types of teeth – 8 incisors at the front, 4 canine next to them, 8 premolars and 12 molars at the rear of the mouth.

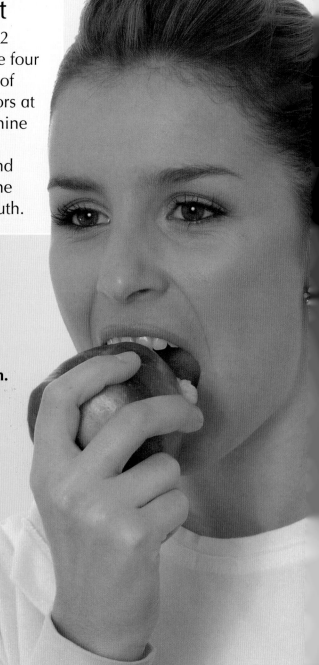

Eating an apple would be difficult without teeth.

Baby teeth

How many teeth you have depends partly on your age. Babies have no teeth or very few. Then, small 'baby', or milk, teeth appear, with most children having a full set of 20 baby teeth by about the age of three or four. From about six or seven years old, these teeth start to fall out and are replaced by adult ones.

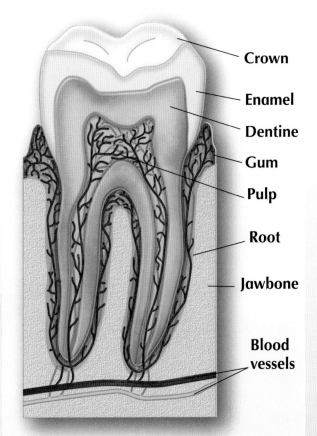

Crown
Enamel
Dentine
Gum
Pulp
Root
Jawbone
Blood vessels

Uses of teeth

Teeth are like tools and have different shapes for different tasks. The chisel-like incisors at the front have straight, narrow edges for biting and slicing food. The canines, or eye teeth, next to the incisors are tall and pointed to tear and rip. The premolars and molars, or cheek teeth, are broad and flat with rounded humps for crushing and chewing.

Inside a tooth

A tooth has two parts – the crown above the gum and the roots below. The top layer of the crown is made of enamel. Beneath this is dentine, which is also a very tough material, and in the middle is the soft pulp. Blood vessels supply the tooth with nutrients.

Hunting teeth

Lions and other hunting animals have very large, pointed canine teeth for stabbing into prey and ripping flesh. Lions also have sharp-edged molar teeth called carnassials for cutting into tough meat.

Canines
Carnassials

119

Chewing and swallowing

After you have taken a bite using the sharp incisor teeth at the front of your mouth (see pages 118–119), your tongue pushes the food around so that it can reach the molar teeth at the back. These crush the food up so that it makes a pulp, which is easier to swallow.

A mushy mess

A liquid called saliva, or spit, helps moisten and soften the food and make it even more squishy. Saliva is made in six glands on the sides of the face, which release up to 1.5 litres a day into the mouth. There is a regular slow release of saliva to keep the mouth and lips moist, but during eating much more saliva flows.

This young girl is learning how to eat, by co-ordinating the movements of her lips, tongue and jaws – it can be a messy business!

Saliva glands

There are three salivary glands located on each side of the face. The parotid gland is just in front of the ear. The submandibular gland is at the back of the lower jaw. The sublingual gland is under the tongue.

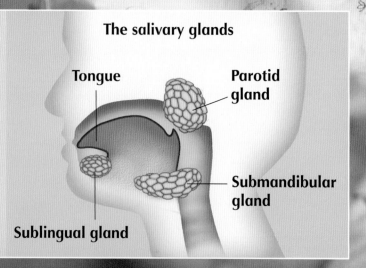

The salivary glands

Tongue

Parotid gland

Submandibular gland

Sublingual gland

Study a swallow

- Stand in front of a mirror and watch and feel your neck carefully.

- Get ready to swallow and feel how your neck muscles tighten.

- As you swallow, see and feel how your upper neck bulges.

- Feel your lower neck as the movement passes downwards and the swallow ends.

Chemical attack

Saliva contains a substance called an enzyme. Enzymes attack food and break it down into more simple chemicals. The enzyme in saliva is known as amylase. It breaks apart starchy substances in food. This is the first of many chemical processes that play a part in digestion.

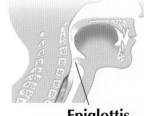

It's Amazing!

An average person bites and chews food more than 1000 times each day. This helps to keep the jaw muscles strong and healthy.

1. Food pushed to back of mouth.

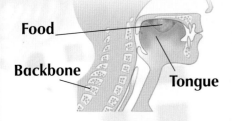

Food

Backbone

Tongue

Swallowing

(1) At the start of swallowing, the tongue separates off part of the mouthful of food and pushes it to the back of the mouth. (2) The back of the tongue forces the food down into the upper throat. (3) The lower throat tightens and a flap – the epiglottis – folds down over the entrance to the trachea. (4) Muscles in the oesophagus 'grab' the food as it passes over the epiglottis. (5) The food begins its journey down the oesophagus.

2. Food reaches upper throat.

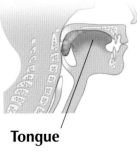

Tongue

3. Epiglottis covers trachea.

4. Food enters oesophagus.

5. Food is swallowed.

Trachea

Epiglottis

Oesophagus

Epiglottis

In the stomach

Swallowed food takes a few seconds to travel down the oesophagus. It is pushed into the bag-like stomach, which attacks the food with powerful acids, enzymes and other chemicals.

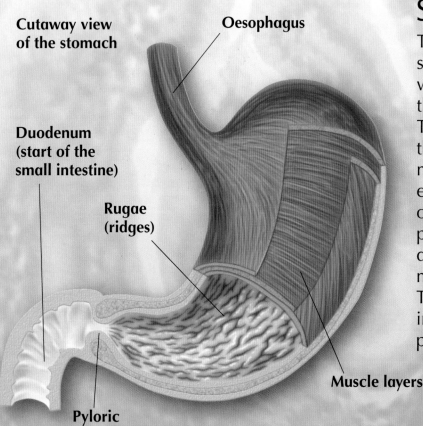

Cutaway view of the stomach

Oesophagus

Duodenum (start of the small intestine)

Rugae (ridges)

Pyloric sphincter

Muscle layers

Stomach wall

The stomach is a large bag that sits just below the left lung. Its walls have several layers – three of these are made of muscle fibres. The muscles tighten and contract the stomach to squash, mix and mash the food inside. The entrance to the stomach from the oesophagus and the exit into the part of the intestine called the duodenum, both have rings of muscle fibres known as sphincters. These stay closed to keep the food in the stomach until it is ready to pass into the intestines.

Stomach wall

The inside of the stomach wall is folded into ridges called rugae, which allow the stomach to stretch. The innermost layer of the stomach wall is the mucosa. The next layer is the tough and stretchy submucosa. The three muscle layers are next, forming the outside of the stomach.

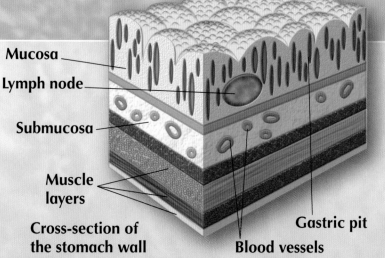

Mucosa

Lymph node

Submucosa

Muscle layers

Gastric pit

Blood vessels

Cross-section of the stomach wall

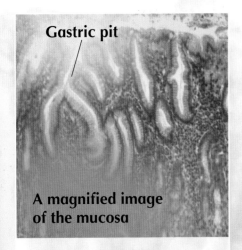

Gastric pit

A magnified image of the mucosa

Gastric pits

The mucosa has thousands of gastric pits. These are lined with cells that make a wide range of chemicals, including slimy mucus, hydrochloric acid and the enzyme pepsin.

Warning! Acid!

Hydrochloric acid is an extremely strong chemical. It is over ten times more powerful than the acidic juices found in vinegar and lemon.

Stomach juices

Apart from mashing the food physically, the stomach also attacks the food with powerful chemicals. Its lining produces a strong acid called hydrochloric acid. The lining also makes more of the chemicals called enzymes. These get to work breaking down different parts of the meal. For example, lipase attacks fatty foods and pepsin breaks down proteins.

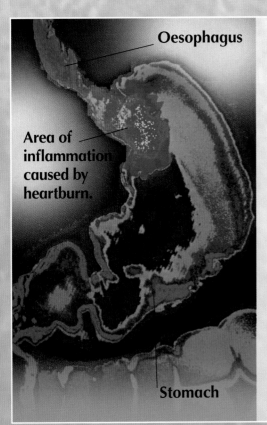

Oesophagus

Area of inflammation caused by heartburn.

Stomach

Heartburn

In some people, the contents of the stomach seep back up into the oesophagus, or lower gullet. This causes inflammation and pain in the chest, where the acid attacks the gullet lining. The pain is known as heartburn, although it has nothing to do with the heart.

An image showing inflammation caused by stomach contents entering the oesophagus.

Top Facts

- Your stomach begins to contract and produce juices as soon as you see or smell food.

- An adult stomach can hold up to 2 litres of food and drink.

- Most food stays in the stomach for one to four hours.

- Fatty foods stay in the stomach for longer.

Guts galore

After a few hours in the stomach, even the most beautiful-looking meal has become a thick, dark, mushy 'soup'. There is more digestion to come, however, in the next part of the digestive tract – the small intestine.

Gut pioneer

In 1780, Italian scientist Lazzaro Spallanzani wrote a book about digestion. He did many experiments on his own digestive system, such as swallowing food in net bags on long pieces of string and pulling them back up to see what had happened.

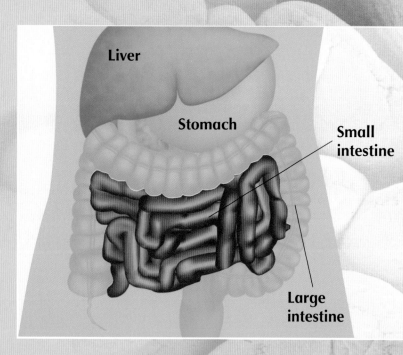

Liver

Stomach

Small intestine

Large intestine

Small intestine

The small intestine, or small bowel, is a narrow but very long tube. It has three parts – first, the duodenum, which is the shortest section, then the middle section, the jejunum, and finally the longest section, the ileum, which connects to the large intestine. The small intestine is coiled, looped and folded into the middle of the lower body and is almost surrounded by the next part of the digestive tract, the large intestine.

More digestion

The small intestine contains many more enzymes that attack food and continue breaking it into smaller pieces. Most of these enzymes are not made in the small intestine but come from another digestive organ called the pancreas, which is found in the left side of the body under the stomach.

A microscopic image of the villi in the lining of the small intestine.

Intestine lining

The small intestine has many folds in its lining. The folds are made of millions of tiny finger-like parts called villi. Each single villus has a system of tiny vessels inside – some are for blood, but a larger one, the lacteal, is for the fluid known as lymph (see pages 104–105). Nutrients pass into the blood and the lymph. The folds and villi give a huge surface area for absorbing nutrients.

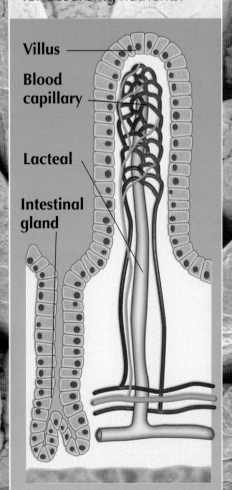

Villus

Blood capillary

Lacteal

Intestinal gland

Taking in

As food reaches its last stages of digestion, the small intestine has another job – it soaks up, or absorbs, the resulting nutrients. These nutrients are small enough to seep through the lining of the small intestine into the blood, which carries them away to the liver.

It's Amazing!

At about 6 metres, the small intestine is the longest part of the digestive tract. If it was straight rather than bent, a person would need to be almost 8 metres tall!

Breaking down food

The diagram on the right shows approximately how long food spends in each part of the intestine. During the food's travels through the guts, different enzymes break down different types of food. For example, only carbohydrates are broken down in the mouth. Carbohydrates and proteins are broken down in the stomach, while fats are mainly broken down in the small intestine.

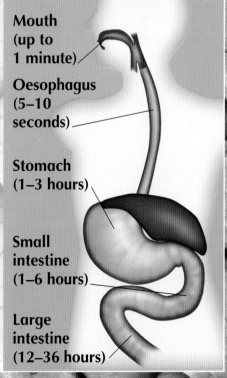

Mouth (up to 1 minute)

Oesophagus (5–10 seconds)

Stomach (1–3 hours)

Small intestine (1–6 hours)

Large intestine (12–36 hours)

On the way out

After digestion and absorption in the small intestine, the next part of the digestive tract is the large intestine. Its main tasks are to take a few more nutrients from the remaining digested food and to remove as much water as the body needs. The waste matter is then ready for removal.

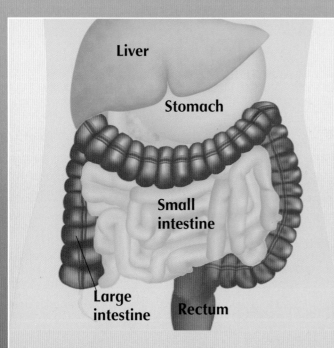

Liver

Stomach

Small intestine

Large intestine

Rectum

Large intestine

At about 1.5 metres long, the large intestine is much shorter than the small intestine, but it is wider – five to six centimetres wide. It forms a type of frame around the abdomen with the small intestine inside it. The large intestine is sometimes called the colon. Its strong muscles push the partly digested food along by contracting and relaxing, creating pulses of movement. The large intestine lining is coated in mucus that lubricates the inside and helps the food move smoothly.

Tiny helpers

The large intestine contains millions of tiny helpers – minute living things of various kinds, mainly bacteria. These microbes are 'friendly' and work with the body. They can digest some things that the body cannot, such as certain plant foods. The microbes use some of these digested products, while the body absorbs the rest. The gut provides the microbes with a safe, warm, moist, food-filled place to live.

Top Facts

- In an average person, more than a half of the faeces, or solid waste, is water. Much of the rest is undigested food material, such as fibre.

- The brown colour of faeces is due to a substance called bilirubin that comes from the breakdown of old red blood cells in the liver.

An X-ray showing a barium meal.

Barium

Inside the large intestine

This X-ray picture was taken after a substance called barium was put into the gut. The barium shows up white on X-rays and helps to reveal the colon.

The final stage

The last part of the large intestine is a short wide tube called the rectum. Faeces collect there before they are finally squeezed out through the anus. This double-ring of muscles loosens to allow the faeces to leave during emptying the bowels, known as defecation.

Treating waste

From the toilet, bodily waste goes through the sewage system to a waste treatment plant. The waste is smelly and can cause disease, so it is treated at the plant to make it harmless.

Tanks of waste at a waste treatment plant.

Young children have no control over going to the toilet, but it is something they learn as they grow up.

Liver and pancreas

The liver and the pancreas are both part of the digestive system although they are not in the digestive tract. The liver is in the upper right abdomen, and the pancreas is to its left, below and behind the stomach.

It's Amazing!

The liver is the largest organ inside the body. In a healthy adult, it weighs an average 1.5 to 2 kilograms. It has the amazing ability to repair and regrow parts of itself if it is injured.

Right lobe

Ligament

Left lobe

Gallbladder

The liver is wedge-shaped and dark red, with a large right lobe and a smaller left one separated by a ligament.

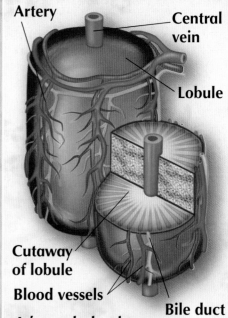

Artery

Central vein

Lobule

Cutaway of lobule

Blood vessels

Bile duct

The liver

The liver has many jobs. One is to make bile, a green fluid that passes to a small storage bag called the gallbladder. When food enters the small intestine, bile flows in and helps to break up fat in the meal. After food is digested and absorbed, nutrients are carried in the blood to the liver, where they are stored, broken down further or sent around the body in the blood.

Liver lobules

The liver has thousands of tiny units, or lobules, that are made up of a central vein surrounded by groups of liver cells. These take in nutrients, make poisons harmless and produce bile.

The pancreas

The pancreas makes digestive juices that flow through a duct into the small intestine. These juices help neutralize the stomach acid so it doesn't burn the gut. They also contain enzymes that help to break down protein, starch and fat in food so that they can be absorbed.

A much magnified image of the islets of Langerhans in the pancreas.

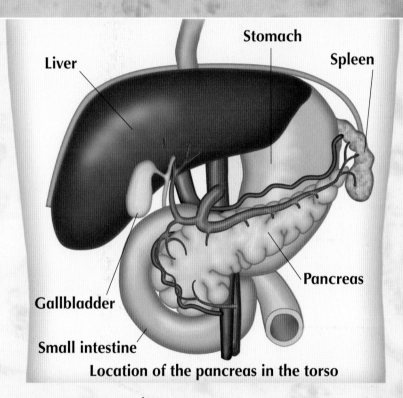

Location of the pancreas in the torso

Liver

Stomach

Spleen

Pancreas

Gallbladder

Small intestine

Hormone maker

The pale pink pancreas is about 20 centimetres long and lies alongside the stomach with the small intestine looping around it. The pancreas contains about one million tiny groups of cells known as islets of Langerhans. These produce messenger chemicals called hormones, two of which are insulin and glucagon, which help to control the blood's level of the sugar glucose. Blood glucose is the body's main source of energy. Surrounding the islets are cell groups called acini, which make the digestive juices.

People with diabetes check their blood glucose level using a special machine.

Sugar levels

Diabetes is an illness in which the body cannot control its blood glucose level properly. It is caused by the body's cells not reacting properly to the hormone insulin.

Filtering blood

Liquid waste – also known as urine – comes from the kidneys, which filter unwanted substances from the blood. The urine is excreted, or released, by the body from the bladder.

Waste removal

As well as delivering nutrients around the body, the blood collects waste and unwanted products from cells and tissue. These waste products are then removed from the blood by the urinary system and excreted as a liquid called urine.

Filtering test

- Stir some salt and ground pepper in a small cup of water.

- Pour the water through a paper towel into another cup. See how the paper traps the larger pepper particles.

- Leave the filtered water to dry up. The salt crystals should be left behind at the bottom. Like the paper, the kidneys filter out some substances, but let others remain.

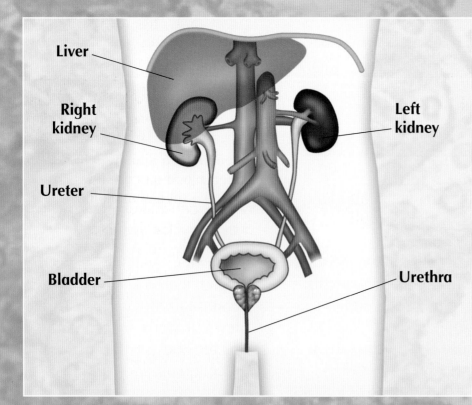

Liver

Right kidney

Left kidney

Ureter

Bladder

Urethra

The urinary system

The urinary system consists of two kidneys at the back of the upper abdomen. From these, two tubes called ureters carry urine down to the bladder – a stretchy bag that holds the urine until it is excreted out of the body. The urine then passes down another tube called the urethra on its way out of the bladder and out of the body.

The urinary system

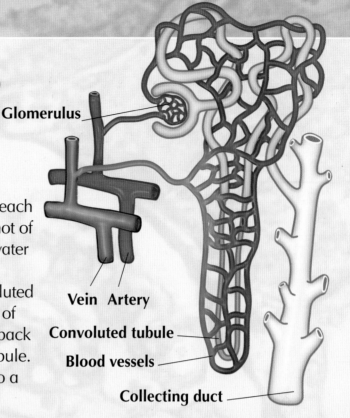

Cutaway of kidney showing nephron.

Glomerulus

Vein   Artery

Convoluted tubule

Blood vessels

Collecting duct

Nephrons

In each kidney, there are about a million microscopic filters called nephrons. Inside each nephron, blood flows through a tangled knot of capillaries called the glomerulus. Waste, water and some useful substances ooze from the glomerulus into a narrow tube – the convoluted tubule. As they flow along the tubule, a lot of the water and useful substances are taken back into the blood in tiny vessels around the tubule. The leftover liquid is urine, which flows into a collecting duct and out of the kidney.

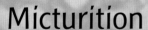

A magnified image of a glomerulus

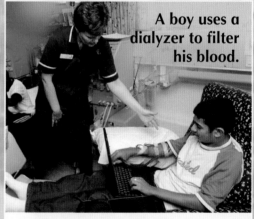

A boy uses a dialyzer to filter his blood.

Micturition

All of the body's blood passes through and is filtered by the kidneys every ten minutes. This means that your blood is filtered about 150 times a day. Once filtered, the urine passes into the bladder. Your bladder can hold about 0.5 litres of urine, although it is stretchy enough to hold twice that amount. However, when there is about 0.2 litres of urine in the bladder, you will feel the need to micturate, or go to the toilet.

Kidney problems

When kidneys become diseased or fail, the blood cannot be filtered properly and waste builds up. A kidney dialysis machine must be used to do the kidneys' job for them. Blood flows along a tube into the machine, where the blood is filtered and waste is removed.

Waste and water

The body is made mostly of water. Some of this water is used to remove waste from the blood, some is lost in sweat and some is breathed out of the lungs as water vapour (see page 84).

Replacing water

Most of the water lost by the body is replaced by water coming into the body as food and drink. Some food, including many fruits and vegetables, contain about 90 per cent water. Most people need to take in more than 2 litres of water a day, but if the weather is hot or if people lead an active lifestyle – which will increase sweating – they will need to take in a lot more. If they do not take in enough water, they may become dehydrated.

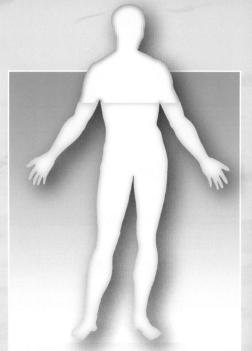

Water levels

The body is between 61 and 64 per cent water. This proportion is higher in children and lower in older people. It varies throughout the day, depending on how much you have eaten or drunk and how hot it is.

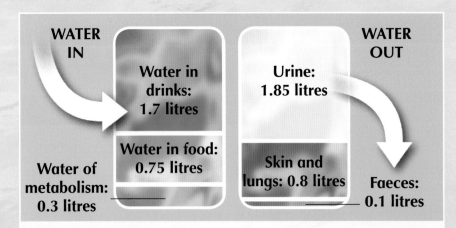

WATER IN

Water in drinks: 1.7 litres

Water in food: 0.75 litres

Water of metabolism: 0.3 litres

WATER OUT

Urine: 1.85 litres

Skin and lungs: 0.8 litres

Faeces: 0.1 litres

Water balance

In a day, your body gains about 2.8 litres of water. Not only does this come from food and drink, but your body also makes water during its chemical activities (see right). Your body also loses about 2.8 litres of water every day.

Top Facts

- Fresh urine does not have much odour but old urine smells of ammonia. This is a gas that is released when bacteria start to break down the urine.

- Urine is mostly water, but it also contains some salts and a chemical called urea.

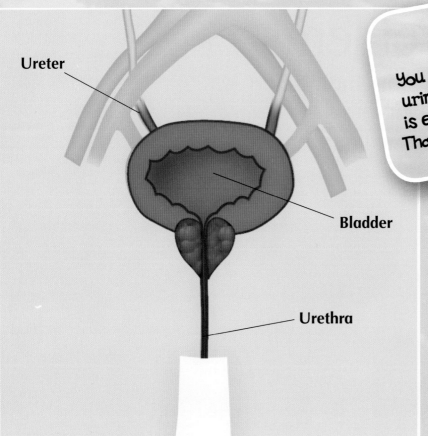

Ureter

Bladder

Urethra

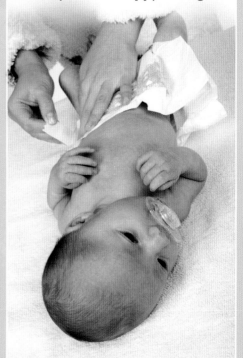

A baby has its nappy changed.

The bladder

When the bladder is empty, it is shrunken and wrinkled. As it fills with urine, its stretchy walls expand and become smoother. Urine trickles into the bladder slowly through the two ureters. To pass urine, or urinate, the ring of muscle around the exit to the bladder relaxes. At the same time, the muscle fibres in the bladder wall tighten to squeeze out the urine.

Making water

One of the ways your body produces water is when it releases energy from nutrients in the blood, such as glucose. The name for all the chemical processes in the body is metabolism, and water made in this way is called 'water of metabolism'.

Urinating

As the bladder fills, stretch sensors in its wall warn us that it is time to use the toilet. Just as babies need to learn how to defecate (see page 127), so they also need to learn how to control the muscles in their bladder and urethra. Until then, they have to wear a nappy.

Digestive problems

Names like 'tummy ache' and 'indigestion' are given to all kinds of abdominal discomfort and pains. These pains are often caused by trapped gas, or wind, from digestion. Conditions such as infections or ulcers are less common and more serious.

A close-up image of a gastric ulcer.

Bowel changes

Diarrhoea occurs when the faeces are watery and runny. It can make the body lose too much water and lead to dehydration. Constipation is when the faeces are hard and dry and may get stuck in the intestine. There are many causes of these conditions, from eating infected food to stress or shock.

Peptic ulcers

A peptic ulcer is a raw, exposed patch of the digestive lining. In the stomach, it is called a gastric ulcer. In the first part of the small intestine, it is called a duodenal ulcer. Most people with peptic ulcers have particular bacteria – *Helicobacter pylori* – in their gut. Peptic ulcers can also be caused by smoking and excessive use of certain drugs, such as aspirin.

Ulcer breakthrough

In 1982, medical scientists John Robin Warren and Barry Marshall discovered a bacterium that may be the cause of peptic ulcers. Before that, many people thought that ulcers were probably caused by consuming too much spicy food, alcohol and caffeine.

A magnified view of salmonella bacteria

Eating too fast

Eating fast without chewing properly can cause problems. Air swallowed with the food can collect in the intestines and cause belching and pain. The food is often too solid to be digested properly, so many of its nutrients are wasted.

It's Amazing!

In the USA, there are around 76 million cases of food-borne illness every single year!

The appendix

The appendix is a small closed tube that sticks out from the first part of the large intestine. It has no role in the digestion process. However, it can become blocked and infected, in which case the appendix will have to be removed.

Large intestine

Appendix

Food poisoning

Food poisoning is an illness that often results in diarrhoea and vomiting, or being sick. It can be caused by germs, such as the bacteria salmonella, entering the body from infected food. Food poisoning can also be caused by eating food that contains poison or harmful chemicals – such as some types of mushroom.

Eating for health

Food is not just something we eat to give our bodies energy. A delicious meal can make us feel happy and relaxed. It is also a chance to sit and talk with family and friends.

It's Amazing!

Eating three apples or two bananas gives the body enough energy to cycle for about an hour!

Healthy food

Experts recommend that everyone eats at least five portions of fruit and vegetables a day. This provides plenty of the vitamins, minerals and fibre needed for a healthy body. A healthy diet should also contain the right amounts of proteins and carbohydrates and even a small amount of fats.

Food will turn bad if it is not stored correctly.

Keep it clean

Always store and prepare food properly. Leaving food out allows germs to land on it and multiply. You should also always wash your hands before preparing or eating food and after using the toilet.

Fresh fruit, such as watermelon, is an important part of a healthy diet.

Meal times

Most people should try to eat three meals, spaced throughout the day. The first meal, breakfast, is especially important as it raises blood glucose levels after a long night with no food. Eating a meal late at night may cause indigestion because the body digests food less well while it is asleep.

A boy visiting the dentist. Teeth need to be checked by the dentist every 6 to 12 months.

Checking ingredients

- Have a look at the packaging on some foods, such as crisps.
- Check the list of ingredients and notice how some contain artificial ingredients and chemicals, such as colourings, flavourings and preservatives.

Tooth care

Teeth need to be brushed at least twice a day to get rid of old bits of food. Without brushing, food can collect on the teeth and attract bacteria, which cause tooth decay, or rotting, as well as gum disease.

BRAIN AND NERVES

The body has many vital parts, but one part – the brain – is at the centre of everything we do, think and remember. The brain is made of billions of microscopic nerve cells with trillions of long, wire-like fibres and connections. More of these cells make up the nerves that snake away from the brain, forming a network that links the brain to all body parts. The brain and nerves together form the nervous system.

Around the brain

The brain, perhaps the most precious body part, is soft and slightly floppy rather like a pink-grey jelly. It is protected against damage by a hard skull bone and by a special cushioning fluid.

Meninges and fluid

The brain sits inside the skull and takes up the top half of the head. Inside the skull, three soft membranes called meninges wrap around the brain. Between the inner two meninges is a layer of liquid known as cerebrospinal fluid, or CSF. Together, the meninges and fluid form a soft cushion around the brain.

Top Facts

- The cushioning fluid flows around and inside the brain.

- There are four fluid-filled chambers called ventricles in the brain.

- The total amount of the cushioning fluid is 120 millilitres – roughly half a mug.

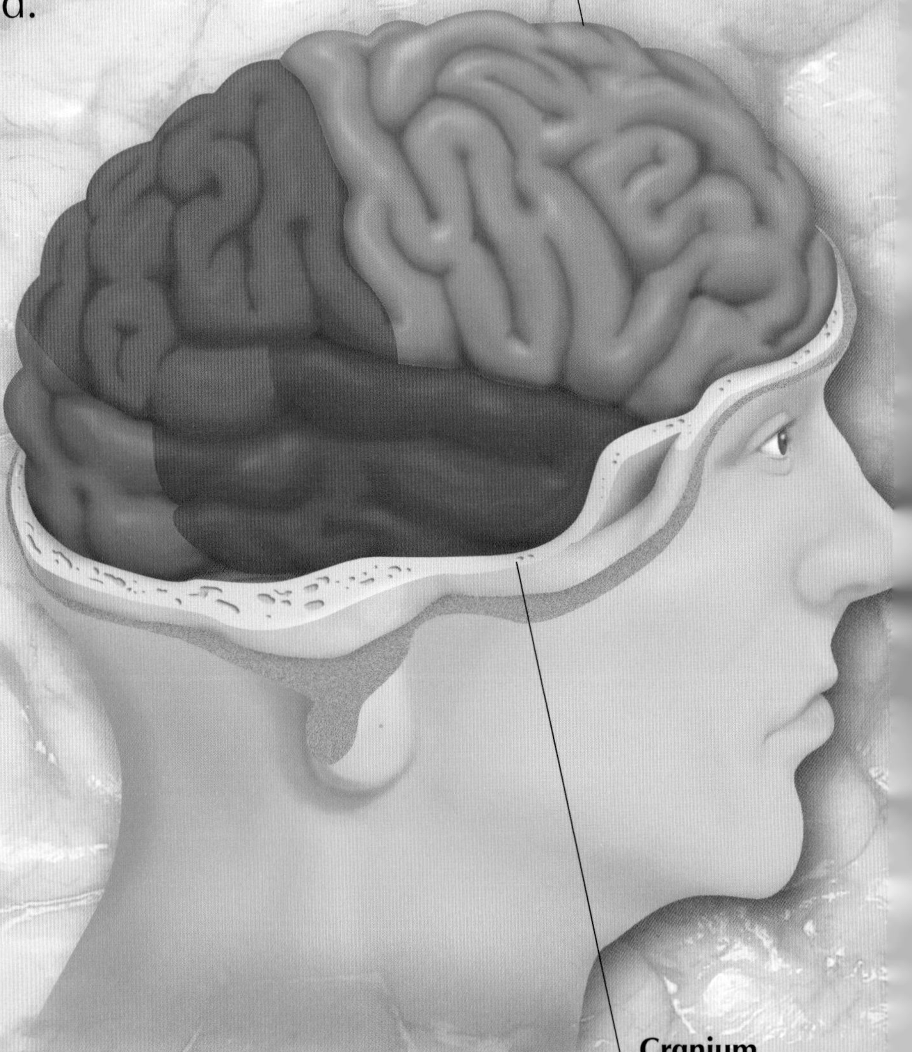

A close-up image showing the wrinkled surface of the brain.

Exterior surface of brain

Cranium (dome of skull bone)

A cutaway of the skull showing the brain and the four lobes of the cerebrum (see page 142).

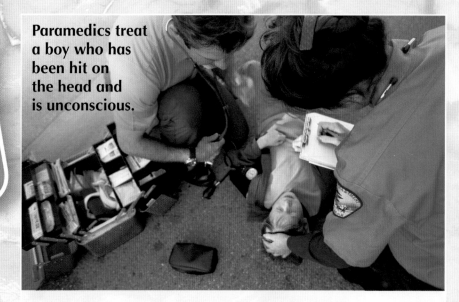

Paramedics treat a boy who has been hit on the head and is unconscious.

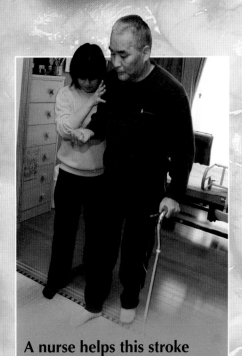

A nurse helps this stroke patient to walk again.

Knock-out

Someone who has been knocked out, or made unconscious, by a blow to the head does not respond or make any movements and seems to be asleep. There may be a brain injury that will require emergency care.

Bone dome

Over and around the brain is the dome of the skull bone called the cranium. This is very strong and guards the brain against knocks and blows. The skin and hair on the head add to this protection and stop the head and brain getting too hot or cold.

Slow recovery

During a stroke, a lack of blood to the brain – perhaps caused by a blocked artery – results in brain cells dying. It may take someone a long time to recover from a stroke because the undamaged parts of the brain have to learn to take over from the damaged parts.

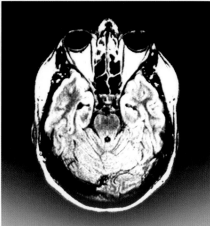

An MRI picture showing a horizontal slice through the middle of the brain.

Seeing inside

A magnetic resonance imaging, or MRI, scanner uses magnetism and radio waves to form an image of thin layers, or slices, of the brain. The images are put together to form a picture of the whole brain to see how it works and to identify any illnesses or problems.

Parts of the brain

The biggest part of the brain is the cerebrum – the large wrinkled dome at the top. This is where most of our thoughts, feelings and ideas take place.

When studying maths, the left side of the brain in these students is very active.

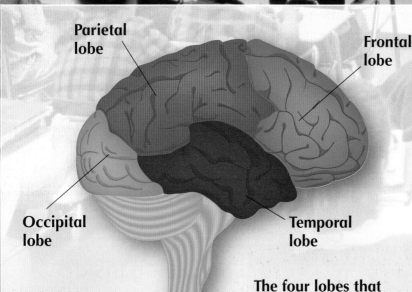

Parietal lobe

Frontal lobe

Occipital lobe

Temporal lobe

The four lobes that make up the cerebrum.

On the outside

The cerebrum makes up about 90 per cent of the brain. It is divided into four regions called lobes, and into left and right halves known as cerebral hemispheres. In most people, the left side of the brain is used for speaking, reading and working out problems. The right side of the brain usually deals with more 'artistic' skills, such as painting and imagination. The wrinkled surface of the cerebrum is a thin layer called the cerebral cortex.

In the middle

The centre of the brain, under the cerebrum, is involved in awareness – monitoring what we see, hear and feel. It also deals with emotions and balance and acts as a relay station. This involves passing messages between the upper and lower brain. It includes parts such as the thalamus and the hypothalamus.

The lower brain

At the lower rear of the brain is a wrinkled lump called the cerebellum. This helps to organize nerve signals going out to the muscles. It helps to make our movements smooth and skilful rather than jerky and clumsy. Like the cerebrum, the cerebellum is divided into two halves; left and right.

The middle of the brain deals with emotions, such as fear.

Emotions

Strong feelings, such as surprise, shock, fear and anger, are based in the hypothalamus. This is also the area involved in powerful urges, like thirst and hunger.

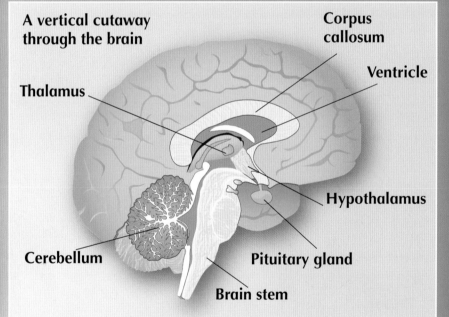

A vertical cutaway through the brain

- Corpus callosum
- Ventricle
- Thalamus
- Hypothalamus
- Cerebellum
- Pituitary gland
- Brain stem

On the inside

A cutaway view of the brain reveals its ventricles, or fluid-filled chambers (shown above shaded in blue). Other parts include the egg-shaped thalamus and the hypothalamus, as well as the corpus callosum, which contains millions of nerve fibres that link the left and right sides of the brain. Below all of these is the brain stem, which controls many of the basic life processes, such as breathing, digestion and blood pressure.

Top Facts

- **The average adult brain weighs 1.4 kilograms.**

- **The largest known normal human brain weighed a whopping 2.9 kilograms.**

- **Bigger brains are not necessarily cleverer. There is no link between the size of a healthy brain and a person's intelligence.**

Sending signals

The brain and nerves contain billions of microscopic nerve cells called neurons. These cells are specialized to receive and send information as tiny pulses of electricity called nerve impulses, or nerve signals.

Dendrite

Nerve cell body

Nerve cells

A typical nerve cell has a wide cell body. Branching from this are many short, thin fingers called dendrites. There is usually also one longer branch called an axon, or nerve fibre. Nerve messages are picked up by the dendrites, processed and altered as they pass around the cell body and then sent on by the axon. A motor nerve carries signals to muscles, telling them when to contract. These signals pass along the axon to the muscle fibres. Surrounding some axons is a thick, fatty protective covering called the myelin sheath.

Axon

Myelin sheath surrounds axon

Electronic circuits enable computers to do millions of calculations a second.

A motor nerve cell

Muscle fibres

Processing power

Nerve cells work in a similar way to the microchips in a computer. Microchips have tiny circuits inside them, along which they send electrical signals.

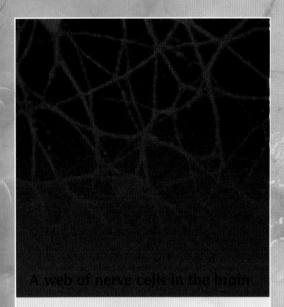
A web of nerve cells in the brain.

Nerve junctions

The dendrites and axons connect to the dendrites and axons of other nerve cells, but they do not actually touch each other. The junctions are separated by tiny gaps called synapses. Nerve messages 'jump' across the synapse – not as electrical signals but in the form of chemicals called neurotransmitters. Each chemical 'jump' takes less than a thousandth of a second.

Nerve web

The brain contains about 100 billion nerve cells. Each of these may be linked to 10,000 or more other nerve cells. The number of connections means there are trillions of pathways for signals to travel between nerve cells.

It's Amazing!

Brain waves can be detected by sensors on the head that can switch a device on or off. These sensors allow some people who are paralyzed to control devices, such as computers, just by thinking.

A patient wired up to an electroencephalogram, which measures brain waves.

Brain machine

In 1924, German physician Hans Berger invented the first machine to measure electrical signals in the human brain. In secret, he tried it out on his son Klaus, then on other people. In 1929, Berger published his first report on the brain's electrical activity.

Brain waves

The brain's electrical signals can be detected by sensor pads on the head. The brain waves, or signals, can then be displayed on a screen or a paper strip as jagged wavy lines. The pattern of waves helps doctors to identify certain brain problems so that they can be treated.

Brain map

The outer layer of the cerebrum is called the cerebral cortex. It contains about half of the brain's nerve cells – about 50,000 million – and the trillions of connections between them.

Bad accident

In 1848, American railway worker Phineas Gage suffered a terrible injury. An iron bar passed through his frontal lobe. Before the injury, Gage was likeable but after the injury, he became difficult and short-tempered. This event started the study of how the brain is involved in personality and behaviour.

A map of the cortex

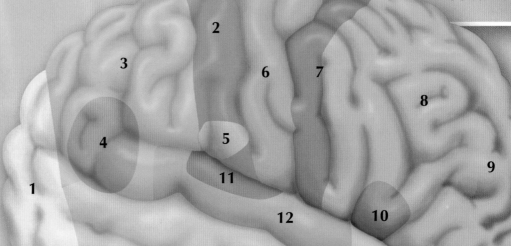

KEY TO BRAIN MAP
1. Visual area (sight)
2. Somatosensory centre (touch)
3. Secondary touch area
4. Posterior (Wernicke's) speech centre
5. Gustatory centre (taste)
6. Motor centre (organizing movements)
7. Premotor centre (planning movements)
8. Frontal cortex (behaviour and personality)
9. Language area (recognizing and understanding words)
10. Anterior (Broca's) speech centre
11. Auditory centre (hearing)
12. Vestibular centre (balance)

Regions of the cortex

The cortex is the main place in the brain where we become aware of what we see, hear, smell, taste and touch – our senses. It is also the place where we plan movements, known as motor skills, and organize them. Each of these sensory and motor processes takes place in a different area of the cortex.

The brain interprets signals sent by the eyes and turns them into pictures.

Seeing

A person who suffers a hard knock to the lower back of the head, where the visual centre is, may have sight problems and 'see stars'.

It's Amazing!

If the cerebral cortex was spread out flat, it would be the size of a pillowcase and almost as thin. But its deep wrinkles allow it to fit neatly inside the head.

Hearing

Nerve signals from each ear pass along nerves to the hearing centre, which is on the temporal lobe. If someone suffers a knock on the head at this place, they sometimes hear buzzing or scratching noises. These sounds do not come from the ear but are 'made up' by the jolted brain.

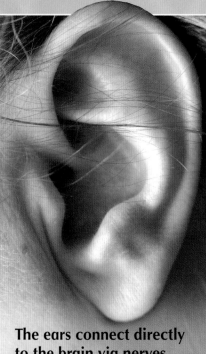

The ears connect directly to the brain via nerves.

The mind

The cortex is the major site for thinking and for general consciousness, or awareness – what we call our 'mind'. The cortex is involved in learning and memory, too. It is sometimes called grey matter because all its nerve cells give it a grey colour. Nerve axons from the cortex's nerve cells pass inwards to the central part of the brain, where they connect to other parts, such as the thalamus and hypothalamus (see page 143).

Personality

Many parts of the brain are involved how we behave, how we feel and what we think. These things make us who we are – our personality. These areas include parts of the cortex, especially the frontal lobe, and the hypothalamus (see pages 142–143). The brain sends signals to your face, maybe telling it to look sad if that's how you feel.

The main nerves

The brain cannot do much at all by itself – it depends on nerves to link it to the rest of the body. There are 25 major nerves carrying signals between the brain, the senses, the muscles and the glands.

Breathing, as this diver is doing underwater, is regulated by the cranial nerves.

Connecting nerves

The 24 cranial nerves are grouped in 12 pairs. They join the brain to various parts, mainly in the head and neck. Some carry signals to the brain and are called sensory nerves. Others carry instructions to the muscles and are called motor nerves.

Olfactory nerve from the nose

Optic nerve from the eye

Oculomotor, trochlear and abducens nerves to eye muscles

Facial nerve to the tongue, for taste, saliva and tear glands

Trigeminal nerve to skin on face

Vestibulocochlear nerve from the ear, for hearing and balance

Glossopharyngeal nerve to rear tongue, for taste

Accessory nerve to voice box

Hypoglossal nerve to tongue, for speaking and swallowing

Vagus nerve to lungs, heart and other organs

Cranial nerves

The sensory nerves bring signals to the brain from the sense organs, such as the eyes and ears. These nerves are the olfactory, the vestibulocochlear and the optic. The motor nerves carry signals from the brain to the muscles and glands. These are the oculomotor, the trochlear, the abducens, the accessory and the hypoglossal. Some nerves carry both sensory and motor signals. They are the vagus, the trigeminal, the facial and the glossopharyngeal.

Some people with spinal injuries use wheelchairs to move around.

Spinal cord

The 25th main nerve, the spinal cord, is the brain's chief link to the rest of the body. It starts at the brain stem and passes down into the body via a tunnel along the inside of the backbone. The bones of the spinal column protect the spinal cord from injury.

Spinal injury

An injury to the neck or back can damage the spinal cord, which may no longer carry signals between the brain and body parts. If the damage is low in the back, it can affect feeling and movement in the legs. If the damage is in the neck, then the arms may also lose feeling and movement.

The squid is very useful for studying how nerves work.

Giant nerves

The squid's main nerve cell has a giant axon – a huge nerve fibre as thick as the lead in a pencil. This can easily be studied, cut, joined and altered to find out how nerves work, how they carry nerve signals and how they can repair themselves.

Top Facts

• Nerve signals pass along the nerves at speeds of up to 120 metres per second.

• The largest nerves can handle about 300 signals every single second.

• A person with a spinal injury who has lost the use of his or her legs is called a paraplegic, while someone who has lost the use of both arms and legs is called a quadriplegic.

Bodywide nerves

The brain and the spinal cord together are known as the central nervous system. The bodywide network of nerves that joins to them and branches out to all body parts is the peripheral nervous system.

Spinal nerves

The spinal cord is about 45 centimetres long and as thick as your little finger. Like the brain, it has meninges and cerebrospinal fluid around it to cushion it from knocks. Pairs of nerves branch left and right from the cord. These nerves connect to muscles, glands, bones, skin, blood vessels and other body parts, reaching right to the ends of your fingers and toes.

Tough nerves

A typical nerve looks like shiny, grey string. It is flexible enough to bend at your joints but tough enough to withstand being squeezed by the muscles around it. Inside the nerve are bundles of axons. The widest nerves are the sciatic nerves, which are the major nerves from the legs and are each as thick as a thumb.

Brain

Cervical (neck) nerves

Spinal cord

Thoracic (upper body) nerves

Radial nerve

Median nerve

Ulnar nerve

Sacral (pelvis) nerves

Femoral (upper leg) nerve

The major nerves of the body

This girl needs quick reaction times when she does karate.

Speedy signals

While the slowest nerve signals travel at about 0.5 metres per second, the fastest can flash from your toes to your brain in less than a fiftieth of a second! The speed of nerve signals limits how fast we can react, for example, in sports. The time it takes to react to something, such as the starting gun in a race, is usually about 0.25 seconds.

Sciatic nerve

Tibial (lower leg) nerve

It's Amazing!

Nerve signals for pain go slower than those for touch. When you stub your toe, you feel your toe touch something, then a split second later you feel the pain.

A doctor tests the knee-jerk reflex by tapping the knee.

Reflexes

Some nerves send signals to the spinal cord, which sends signals back without involving the brain. The result is an automatic reaction called a reflex. Doctors check reflexes to make sure nerves are working properly.

Testing your eyes

- In a well-lit room, look at one of your eyes in a mirror and notice the size of the pupil Close both eyes for 10 seconds.
- The instant you open them, watch the pupil carefully. As soon as the eyes open, the pupils get smaller. This is a reflex (see page 167).

Thinking, learning and memory

What is a thought, and where does it happen? Our thoughts and ideas are sets of nerve signals flashing around different pathways in the brain, especially in the cortex.

Children learning in class. Facts that you learn go into your memory.

Learning

When we learn something, we form a memory of it. Like thoughts, memories are certain pathways of nerve signals called memory traces. To learn something, nerve cells form synapses, or new connections, to create a new memory trace. There are two types of memory – short-term and long-term. Short-term memory involves memories that are only stored for just 30 seconds, while long-term memories are remembered for much longer.

Where are memories kept?

There is no single memory centre in your brain. Some aspects of a memory are stored in the prefrontal part of the cerebral cortex, and some in other brain areas, such as the amygdala. The hippocampus helps to store important memories for a long time.

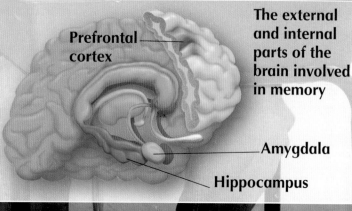

Prefrontal cortex

The external and internal parts of the brain involved in memory

Amygdala

Hippocampus

So many memories

Memory is not only used for lists of facts. We remember people's names, events such as birthdays and holidays, how to carry out skilled movements and many other things. In some ways, memories are like muscles. The more they are used, the stronger they stay. Recalling a memory means that signals pass around the memory trace, refreshing the connections.

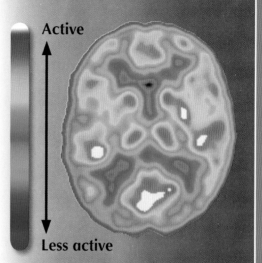

Active

Less active

A PET scan of a cross-section of the brain showing the active areas during a brain stimulation test.

It's Amazing!

For its size, the brain uses 10 times more energy than other body parts. The brain uses 20 per cent of the body's total energy supply.

Busy brain

PET (positron emission tomography) scans show which parts of the brain are active during a task or when learning something. The busiest brain parts 'light up' because their nerve cells are very active and use more energy.

Memory games

Look at the objects above for 20 seconds and then close the book and try to remember as many as you can. You will probably be able to recall some of them. By using some of the tricks described on the right, you may recall more and remember them for longer.

Memory tricks

- In the game on the left, write down the first letter of the name of each object and arrange the letters into a new word.
- Or invent a story that includes the objects.
- Or try grouping them according to their colours. These 'tricks' should help to improve your memory.

153

Good night's sleep

For about a third of our lives, we are not aware of our brains at all – this is when we are asleep. But scientific studies of sleeping people show that the brain is busy all night.

Body and brain

The heartbeat and breathing slow down during sleep. So do digestion and urine production. Most muscles relax. Some processes, however, speed up. Our bodies mend the everyday wear and tear in cells and tissues more quickly at night.

During sleep, most people move about quite a lot. This stops nerves and blood vessels from being squashed.

Sleep cycle

The first part of a night's sleep is deep sleep (stage 4). After an hour or two, sleep becomes lighter, the eyes move and breathing speeds up. This is REM (rapid eye movement) sleep (stage 1), when dreams occur. Periods of deep and light sleep follow, with the deep sleep becoming shallower (stages 3 and 2) towards morning.

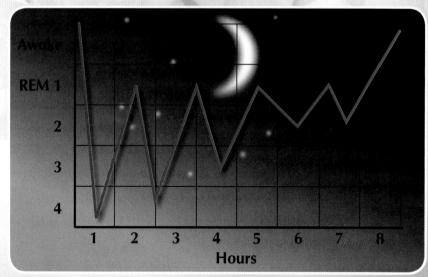

A graph of the different stages of sleep during the night

It's Amazing!

In 1964, American student Randy Gardner stayed awake for 11 days, which is a world record. But going without sleep can be very harmful (see right).

Jet lag

Sleeping occurs in a natural 24-hour rhythm due to the 'body clock', which based in a tiny part the brain. Your body clock is affected by daylight and darkness. When you travel long distances quickly your body clock can get confused – this is known as jet lag.

Losing sleep

Exactly what the brain does during sleep is not clear. It may be sorting through the day's events and deciding what to remember or forget. Some people are unable to sleep during the night. This is called insomnia. A lack of sleep can cause tiredness, headaches, confusion, slowed reactions and many other problems. Serious lack of sleep is linked to accidents, infections and other illnesses.

Night shift

Some people work at night, when most of us are asleep. If this happens regularly, the body and brain gradually adjust their sleeping and eating times and settle into a new routine. But switching quickly between daytime and night-time working has been linked to various health problems.

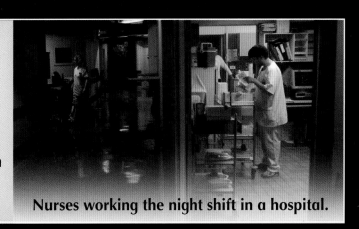

Nurses working the night shift in a hospital.

Automatic body

Many things, such as the heartbeat and digestion, happen in the body all the time. We do not have to think about them. These involuntary actions are carried out by the autonomic nervous system.

Involuntary control

We cannot control the autonomic nervous system. Usually, we are not even aware of it. Breathing is an exception – it is mainly involuntary because we do not have to remember to take each breath, but we can also alter breathing at will, for example, to blow up a balloon.

Top Facts

- The chief control centre in the brain for the autonomic system is the hypothalamus, which links to several centres located in the brain stem.

- The hypothalamus also links to the cerebral cortex, the amygdala and the hippocampus to control responses, such as fear.

A person connected to a life support machine. This controls many of the actions of the autonomic nervous system if it becomes damaged.

Exercising in a gym will raise a person's heart rate.

Heart rate

We are sometimes aware of our heartbeat changing, such as during exercise. The rate is controlled partly by nerve signals from the heart-rate centre in the brain stem – which go along the vagus nerve to the heart – and partly by chemicals called hormones (see pages 158–159).

Autonomic nervous system

The autonomic system has two part parts – the sympathetic and parasympathetic. The sympathetic part (in red below) uses spinal nerves and long, chain-like parts called autonomic ganglia on either side of the spinal cord. It speeds up or stimulates body parts. The parasympathetic (in blue below) uses mainly cranial and sacral (lower back) nerves and slows down or relaxes body parts.

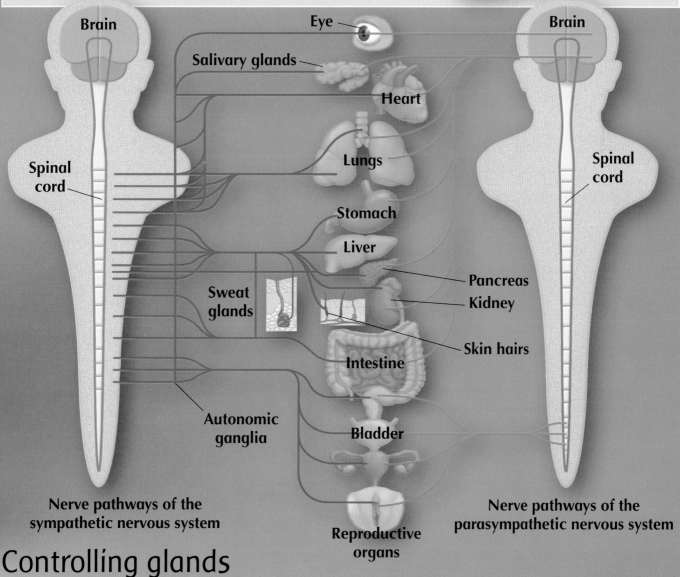

Brain

Eye

Salivary glands

Heart

Spinal cord

Lungs

Stomach

Liver

Pancreas

Kidney

Sweat glands

Skin hairs

Intestine

Autonomic ganglia

Bladder

Brain

Spinal cord

Reproductive organs

Nerve pathways of the sympathetic nervous system

Nerve pathways of the parasympathetic nervous system

Controlling glands

The activities of the glands are controlled by the autonomic system. Examples of these involuntary actions are the salivary glands releasing saliva when we eat and the stomach releasing digestive juices when food reaches it.

Chemical control

The brain and nerves, which send information as tiny electrical signals, are not the body's only control system. A second system also organizes and controls body parts and processes. It is not electrical but chemical and is called the endocrine, or hormonal, system.

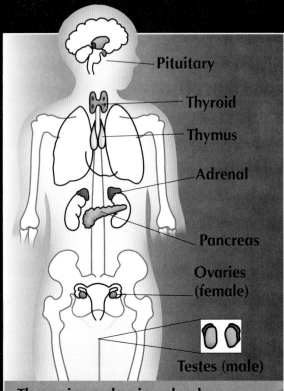

Pituitary

Thyroid

Thymus

Adrenal

Pancreas

Ovaries
(female)

Testes (male)

The major endocrine glands

Hormone glands

Various glands around the body form the endocrine system. These glands make chemicals called hormones and release them into the blood.

Hormones

Different hormones affect different parts of your body. Hormones released by the thyroid gland in the neck control the rate of many chemical processes in the body. Adrenal hormones affect the production of urine and how you cope with stress. Hormones from the pancreas regulate the level of sugar in the blood.

Growth hormone is made in the pituitary. Higher levels of it make the body grow taller, which is very useful in sports, such as basketball.

Diabetes pioneers

In 1921 in Canada, Frederick Banting and Charles Best discovered insulin – a hormone made by the pancreas. They also found that animal insulin could be used to treat diabetes, a condition in which the body cannot control the levels of sugar found in the blood.

It's Amazing!

Laughter is good for you because it can reduce the levels of stress hormones, such as adrenaline, in your body, making you more relaxed.

During a bungy jump, the body produces adrenaline as it reacts to the danger. Some people enjoy this 'adrenalin rush'.

Adrenaline rush

The adrenal glands make adrenaline, which gives the body a burst of energy by increasing the heart rate and flow of blood. This allows the body to react quickly to danger or stress, either by running away or facing it – this is known as 'flight or fight'.

The speed of control

There are more than 30 main hormones in your body and these control processes that happen fairly slowly – in hours, days or even years. These processes include growth, digestion and making urine. In contrast, the processes the nerves control happen much faster – usually in seconds or minutes.

Nerves and hormones

The pituitary makes more than ten hormones, many of which control other endocrine glands. For example, it releases a hormone that stimulates the ovaries to produce eggs. The pituitary is linked by blood vessels and nerves to the hypothalamus and the brain. Using these links, the nervous and hormonal systems work together to make the body function normally.

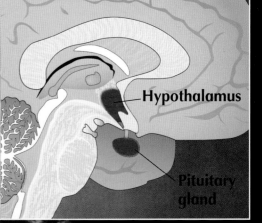

Location of hypothalamus and pituitary gland in the brain

Hypothalamus

Pituitary gland

Brain and nerve problems

The brain and nerves do such important jobs that problems with them can be serious. Most people, however, just experience minor problems, such as mild headaches.

Funny feelings

Sometimes, when we sit or lie in an awkward position we get a strange tingling feeling called 'pins and needles'. This is usually due to squashing a nerve, which means it cannot carry signals. When this happens, we cannot feel or move the body part. Bending, stretching and rubbing the part soon cures the problem.

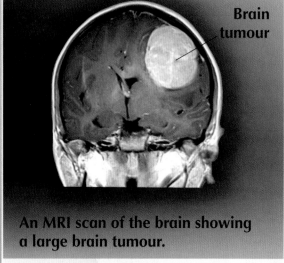

Brain tumour

An MRI scan of the brain showing a large brain tumour.

A woman about to have an MRI scan – the machine will produce images of her brain.

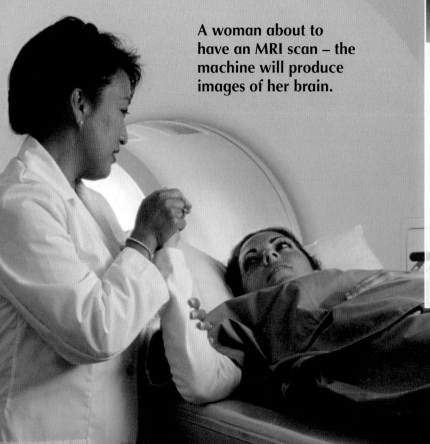

Brain tumours

Occasionally, a tumour, or growth, forms inside the brain. As it grows, it squashes the brain within the skull. The pressure can cause headaches and loss of feeling and movement in certain body parts, as well as vision problems and mood swings. It may be possible to cut a hole in the skull and remove the tumour.

Meningitis

Bacteria and viruses can infect the layers around the brain – the meninges. This illness is called meningitis and it causes a severe headache and other symptoms, such as a stiff neck and skin rash. Meningitis is serious and requires emergency treatment.

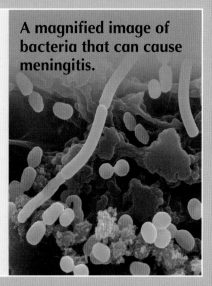

A magnified image of bacteria that can cause meningitis.

Brain doctors

- More than 2300 years ago, Greek doctor Hippocrates described the condition of epilepsy and said it was based in the brain.
- In the 1930s, some doctors used electric shocks to the brain to treat severe brain problems. Treatment such as this is very rare today.

Electrical storm

Epilepsy is a condition in which nerve signals in the brain are disturbed. Some forms of epilepsy involve short periods of 'daydreaming' or making odd movements, such as chewing. In other forms, the person loses consciousness and makes jerky movements called convulsions. Drugs can usually control the problem.

It's Amazing!

In ancient times, people used sharp stones to drill through the skull into the brain, perhaps in an attempt to cure bad headaches. Some people even survived this 'treatment'!

Headaches and migraines

The brain has no pain sensors and cannot feel pain. Headaches usually come from parts around the brain, such as the meninges, blood vessels and muscles. There may be many causes, including infections and stress. Migraines are severe headaches that keep coming back. Doctors are not sure what causes them.

Almost all people get headaches at some time, but most are not serious.

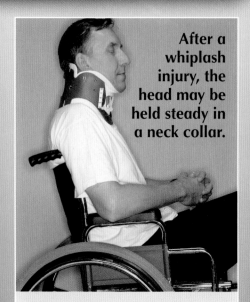

After a whiplash injury, the head may be held steady in a neck collar.

Guarding the brain

The brain is well protected by the meninges, cerebrospinal fluid and skull. But if we do risky activities, such as cycling or rock climbing, it makes good sense to give the brain extra protection.

Whiplash

A car accident may cause the head to 'whip' backwards and forwards on the neck. This can bruise and damage the spinal cord and nerves, causing pain and spasms as well as some temporary loss of movement and feeling in the body. This is called whiplash.

Slow to heal

Nerve cells are very delicate and specialized, and they grow thousands of complex links and connections over many years. If nerve cells are damaged, they are very slow to mend, and sometimes they are not able to repair themselves at all. That is why preventing injuries to the brain and nerves is so important.

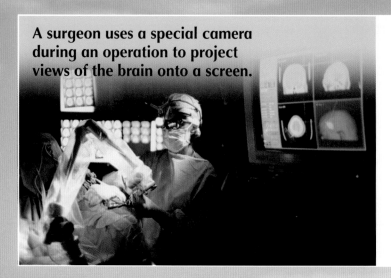

A surgeon uses a special camera during an operation to project views of the brain onto a screen.

Brain surgery

Doctors use special saws, drills and other equipment to open a flap of bone in the skull and expose the brain beneath. Long, thin probes or needles can be pushed deep into the brain to carefully remove diseased tissue or take samples for analysis.

Shields and guards

Nerves are especially at risk of being damaged where they pass through joints. Joint guards on the elbows and knees help to reduce the risk. If a body part is cut off in an accident, doctors may be able to reconnect it using microsurgery. This is when muscles, blood vessels and even nerve fibres are rejoined under a microscope.

Wearing a helmet and other protective gear is essential when riding a motorbike.

It's Amazing!

Staying unconscious for a long time, usually after an accident, is called a coma. In 2003, American Terry Wallis, who was 39, woke up after 19 years in a coma. His first word was "Mom".

Growing nerves

Medical researchers are looking for ways to help repair damaged nerves. Some chemicals, known as neuronal growth factors, encourage nerve cells to lengthen their fibres and send out new connections. Special cells in the nose may have the potential to regenerate into new nerve cells if transplanted into the spine.

A test tube of nerve cells taken from the nose.

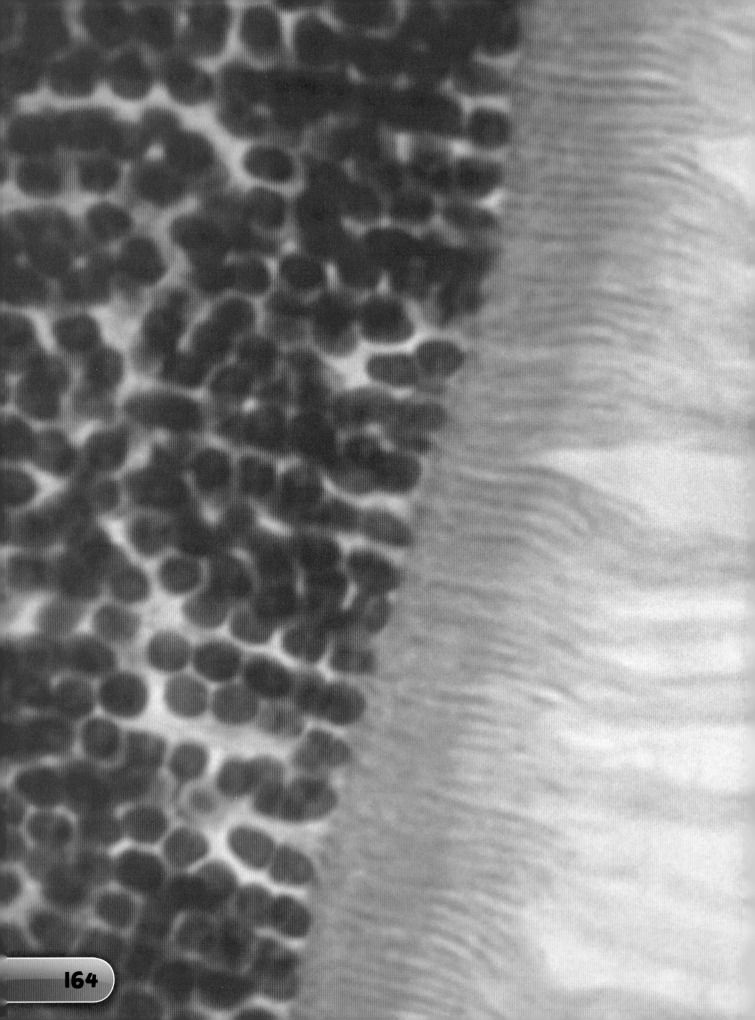

THE SENSES

Can you remember an exciting event such as a theme-park ride, carnival or music show? Take a moment to recall the bright lights, the sounds of the people, machines and music, and the things you touched. You might also remember the different smells that were in the air and perhaps the taste of a snack or treat. Your body's sensory systems – sight, hearing, smell, taste and touch – allow you to experience all these wonderful things.

The eyes

It is thought that over half of the information in our brains comes through our eyes – as words, photographs, drawings, real-life scenes and images on screens.

Ball and socket

Each eyeball is protected by an orbit, or eye socket – a cone-shaped cavity in the skull. The eyeball is ball-shaped and measures about 25 millimetres across. Only about an eighth of the eyeball is visible at the front.

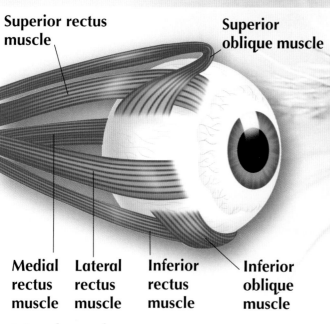

Superior rectus muscle

Superior oblique muscle

Medial rectus muscle

Lateral rectus muscle

Inferior rectus muscle

Inferior oblique muscle

Moving the eye

Six long, slim, ribbon-like muscles join to different parts of the eyeball. Working as a team, these move the eyeball to look up or down and left or right. The eye muscles are among the fastest-reacting in the body.

It's Amazing!
The eye grows less than any other part from birth to adulthood. It is already about 70 per cent of its adult size at birth. This is why babies seem to have such big eyes.

Sclera

Iris

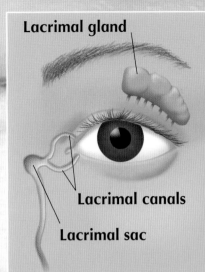

Lacrimal gland

Lacrimal canals

Lacrimal sac

Making tears

Tear fluid is made in the lacrimal glands above each eyeball. Tears smear over the surface of the eyeball with each blink and wash away dust and germs. They then flow through two tubes to a pouch called the lacrimal sac and into the nose.

A crying baby.

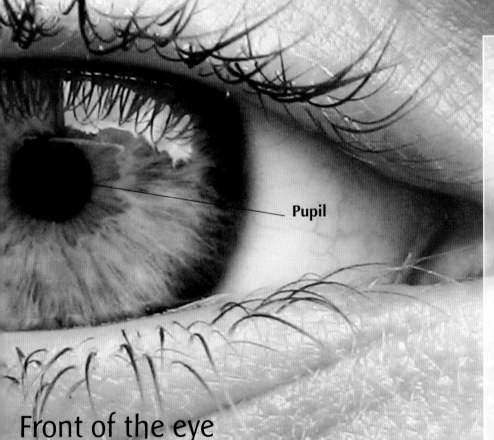

Pupil

Normal light

Bright light

Dim light

Front of the eye

The most noticeable part of the eye is a ring of muscle called the iris, which varies in colour from person to person. In the middle is the pupil, which looks like a black dot but is actually a hole that lets light into the eye's interior. Around the iris is the white of the eye – a tough outer covering of the eyeball called the sclera.

Pupil response

The muscles of the iris relax or contract to change the size of the pupil. The pupil widens in dim light to let in as much light as possible. In bright light, the pupil narrows to prevent too much light entering.

How we see

The eyes turn light rays into nerve signals that go to the brain. The visual centre at the back of the brain is where we recognize and understand what we see (see pages 146–147).

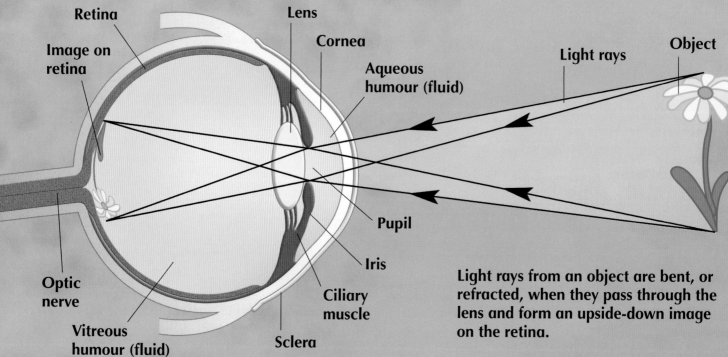

Retina

Image on retina

Optic nerve

Vitreous humour (fluid)

Sclera

Ciliary muscle

Iris

Pupil

Aqueous humour (fluid)

Cornea

Lens

Light rays

Object

Light rays from an object are bent, or refracted, when they pass through the lens and form an upside-down image on the retina.

Into the eye

Light passes through a clear dome called the cornea at the front of the eye and through the pupil into the lens. The ciliary muscles around the lens pull it to change its shape. This alters how much the light rays bend as they pass through the lens, bringing the image into focus on the retina.

Cataracts

A cataract is when the eye lens becomes cloudy, making it hard to see. Cataracts are caused by a number of things, such as a thickening of the lens in old age, exposure to too much heat or conditions inherited from parents.

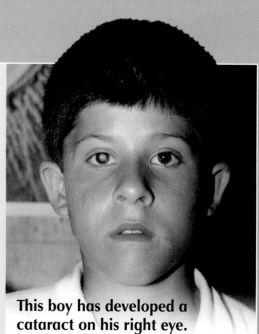

This boy has developed a cataract on his right eye.

Top Facts

- The retina has more than 120 million rod cells and 7 million cone cells.

- Most of the cones are in a small pit at the back of the retina called the fovea. This is where light is focused by the lens to give the clearest, most detailed view of an object.

- Rods are located mainly around the sides of the retina.

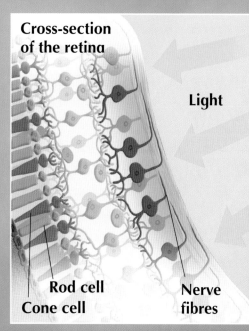

Cross-section of the retina

Light

Rod cell
Cone cell

Nerve fibres

The retina

The retina contains millions of cells called rods and cones. Rod cells work in dim light but cannot pick out colours. Cone cells can detect colours but only work in bright light. When light rays fall on the retina, these cells produce nerve signals, which pass out of the eye through the optic nerve.

Sending signals

The optic nerves carry the nerve signals through the head to the visual centre at the back of the brain. Here, the brain interprets these signals, turns the images the right-way round and produces the pictures that we see.

Tricking the eye

Drawings called optical illusions, such as the ones shown here, are said to trick the eye. In fact, the eye simply records what it sees in a scene. It is the brain that works out what we see by processing and comparing the image to information in its memory. So really, optical illusions trick the brain not the eye.

The impossible cube

Are the centre circles the same size?

The ears

We do not hear with the ears on the sides of our head. These are simply flaps of skin and cartilage. Sounds are changed to nerve signals by a part inside the ear called the cochlea.

A diagram of the ear, showing the outer ear and a cutaway of the middle and inner ear.

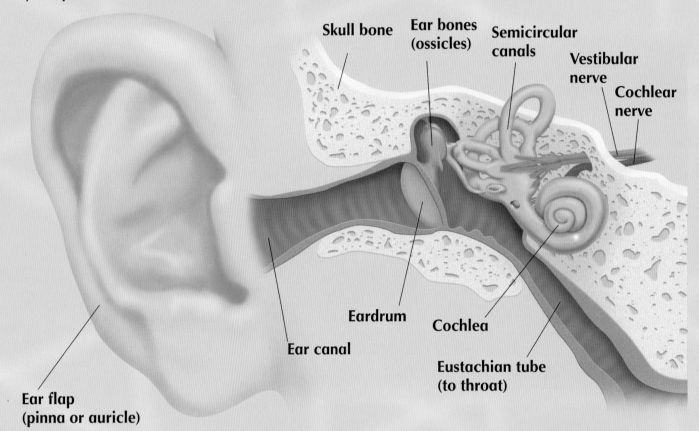

Skull bone

Ear bones (ossicles)

Semicircular canals

Vestibular nerve

Cochlear nerve

Eardrum

Cochlea

Ear canal

Eustachian tube (to throat)

Ear flap (pinna or auricle)

Ear flaps

The ear flaps help to gather sound waves from the air and guide them into the ear canal. Their shape also helps to keep dust, dirt and other objects out of the ear. The canal's lining of wax also traps dust.

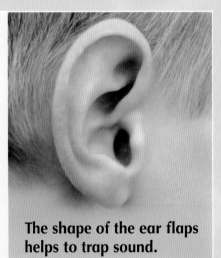

The shape of the ear flaps helps to trap sound.

Parts of the ear

The ear has three main sections. The outer ear is the ear flap on the side of the head and a tube – the ear canal – leading from it. The middle ear is the eardrum at the end of the ear canal and three tiny ear bones. The inner ear is the snail-like cochlea and the semicircular canals.

A look in the ear

Medical staff can check for ear infections or other problems by shining a light from an otoscope into the ear canal. The ear lobe is usually pulled gently to make the ear canal straighter to reveal the eardrum with the ear bones behind it.

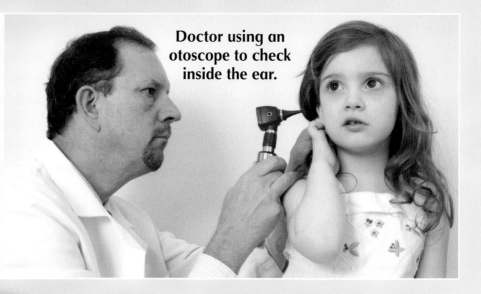

Doctor using an otoscope to check inside the ear.

It's Amazing!

Some animals, such as dogs and bats, can hear sounds that humans cannot detect. Some dog whistles seem to make no noise, but dogs can hear them!

Noticing sounds

Almost nowhere is truly silent. There are usually sounds of some kind – distant traffic, humming machinery, people talking, birds singing or the wind. Much of the time we ignore these sounds because they tell us nothing new. The ears receive them, but our conscious thoughts do not register them. Only when we hear something new, important or exciting do we turn our attention to listening.

A bat-eared fox has huge ear flaps, which it uses to locate insects to eat.

Direction of sound

Many animals have large ears that can be turned to locate a sound. Humans work out the direction of a sound by hearing if the sound is louder on one side of the head than the other, and if a sound arrives at one ear before the other – even if this difference is a fraction of a second.

Top Facts

- A sound's pitch – whether it sounds high or low – is measured in hertz.

- Human ears can hear a range of sounds, from low sounds at about 25 hertz to very high sounds at about 20,000 hertz.

How we hear

Sound waves are vibrations in the air. The process of hearing starts when these waves reach the ear and enter the ear canal.

Into the middle ear

The ear canal carries the sound waves to the eardrum – a thin, tightly stretched membrane, which vibrates as sound waves bounce off it. The eardrum is attached to the ear bones, called ossicles. The vibrations cause the eardrum and the ear bones to vibrate.

Listen to your ear

- Place your hands over your ears. Can you hear a rushing or whooshing noise?
- This is made by sound waves bouncing around between your hands, ear flaps, the inside of your ear canal and your eardrum.

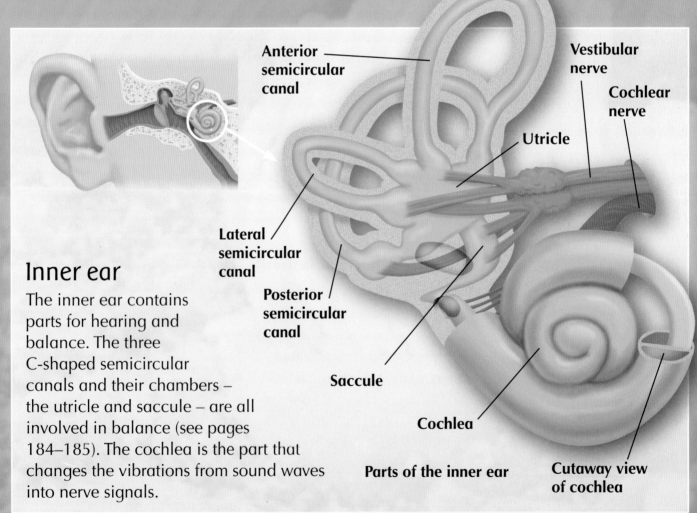

Anterior semicircular canal

Vestibular nerve

Cochlear nerve

Utricle

Lateral semicircular canal

Posterior semicircular canal

Saccule

Cochlea

Parts of the inner ear

Cutaway view of cochlea

Inner ear

The inner ear contains parts for hearing and balance. The three C-shaped semicircular canals and their chambers – the utricle and saccule – are all involved in balance (see pages 184–185). The cochlea is the part that changes the vibrations from sound waves into nerve signals.

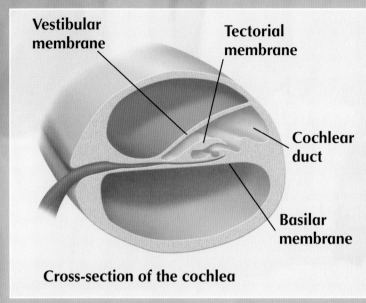

Vestibular membrane

Tectorial membrane

Cochlear duct

Basilar membrane

Cross-section of the cochlea

Inside the cochlear

The cochlea is a tube that is wound into a spiral like a snail's shell. Inside are three fluid-filled ducts, or chambers, which are separated by membranes. The basilar, or lower, membrane has rows of tiny hair cells on it. As the ear bones send waves through the fluid in the cochlea, the micro-hairs on these hair cells push into the tectorial membrane just above and bend as they do so. This makes the hair cells produce nerve signals.

Sounds to signals

As the ear bones vibrate, they send waves through the liquid inside the cochlea. These waves move tiny hairs inside the cochlea, which convert these movements into nerve signals. The signals pass along nerves to the auditory centre in the brain (see page 146) which interprets the signals and turns them into the sounds we hear.

It's Amazing!

The cochlea is the part of the ear that changes sounds to nerve signals. Yet it is only about 5 millimetres high and 9 millimetres wide. It could easily fit on your little fingernail.

Micro-hairs

There are 15,000 to 20,000 hair cells in the cochlea. Each hair cell has 50 to 100 micro-hairs sticking up from it. Vibrations of different speeds (frequencies) make different parts of the basilar membrane shake. The hair cells produce different nerve signals depending on the frequency.

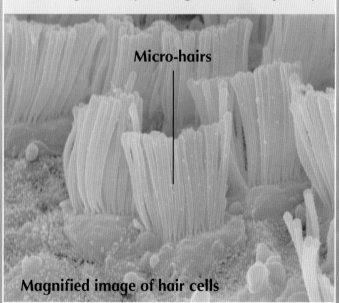

Micro-hairs

Magnified image of hair cells

Nose and smell

Smell and taste are both known as chemosenses. This means that they detect chemical substances in the form of tiny particles too small to see. The nose reacts to smelly particles, called odorants, floating in the air.

Sniff, sniff

Odorant particles floating in the air drift into the nose as air is breathed in. They are detected by two olfactory patches in the roof of the nasal chamber. Sniffing something makes air swirl around inside the nose, which brings more odorant particles higher into the nasal chamber, where they touch the olfactory patches.

A flower produces odorant particles to attract insects so that it can pollinate.

It's Amazing!
The human nose is so sensitive that it can tell the difference between about 10,000 different scents.

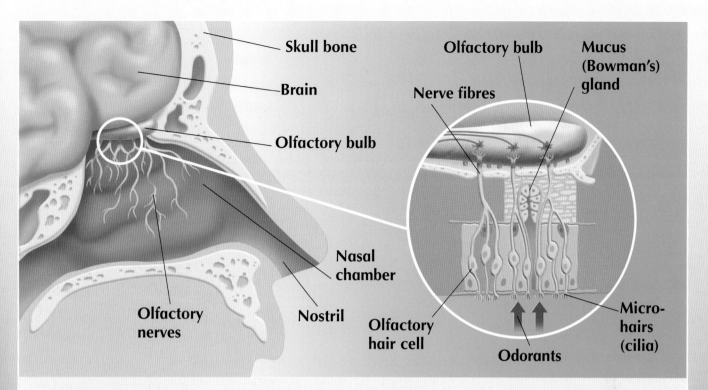

Skull bone

Brain

Olfactory bulb

Nasal chamber

Nostril

Olfactory nerves

Olfactory hair cell

Odorants

Nerve fibres

Olfactory bulb

Mucus (Bowman's) gland

Micro-hairs (cilia)

Inside the nose

The two nostrils lead into the nasal chamber – the air space inside the nose. Each olfactory patch in the roof of the nasal chamber contains about 10 million olfactory hair cells. These hair cells have about 10 to 20 micro-hairs each. The micro-hairs point down into the thick layer of slimy mucus that lines the inside of the nasal chamber.

A close-up of an olfactory patch, where smells are turned into nerve signals.

Smell receptors

Odorant particles seep into the mucus coating the nasal chamber. They come into contact with the micro-hairs of the olfactory hair cells, and these create nerve signals. The signals are sent to the brain via the olfactory bulb. The brain interprets these signals as the aromas we smell.

Useful smells

The brain matches a smell to information it has stored about smells. For example, a wine taster can tell what type of wine he or she is about to drink just by sniffing it – and can even tell the year it was made.

A wine taster smelling wine.

Tongue and taste

The tongue works in a similar way to the nose. It detects substances called flavorants in foods and drinks, using tiny taste buds located in bumps called papillae on its surface.

Tongue's surface

The tongue has groups of small, pimple-like papillae on its surface, which make it rough so it can grip food. The largest ones are vallate papillae at the rear of the tongue. Other types are the long foliate papillae, the thread-like filiform papillae and the mushroom-shaped fungiform papillae.

It's Amazing!

Over the years, some taste buds die and are not replaced. This means that younger people are more sensitive to taste than older people.

Taste buds

Scattered along the upper sides, tip and back of the tongue are about 10,000 taste buds. Each contains 20 to 30 gustatory (taste) hair cells, whose micro-hairs stick up into a taste pore in the tongue's surface. Flavorants attach to these hairs and make the hair cells produce nerve signals.

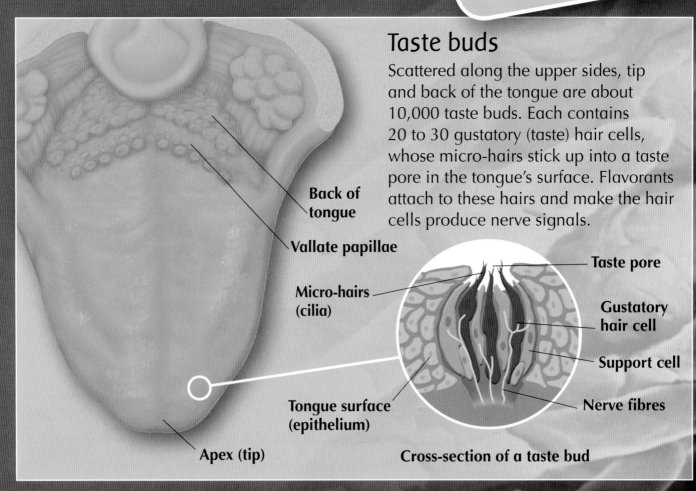

Back of tongue

Vallate papillae

Micro-hairs (cilia)

Tongue surface (epithelium)

Apex (tip)

Taste pore

Gustatory hair cell

Support cell

Nerve fibres

Cross-section of a taste bud

Tasting food

The taste buds work in a similar way to the olfactory patches in the nose. They send nerve signals to the gustatory centre in the brain (see page 146), which works out what flavour you are tasting. Your senses of taste and smell work together to determine the flavour. If you have a cold that has blocked your nose, you may notice that the food you seems to have less taste. It has the same taste, but less smell, and so less overall flavour.

Vallate papilla

Magnified view of tongue papillae

Filiform papilla

Strong flavours

You can sense many different flavours. These are usually grouped into five categories – sweet, salt, sour, bitter and savoury (also called umami) – but there may be more, including spicy flavours such as those found in chillies.

Chillies produce a chemical that burns the tongue.

New thinking

For many years, it was thought that different parts of the tongue sensed different flavours. Recent research shows that most parts of the tongue detect most flavours, except for the central part of the tongue, which has no taste buds.

Skin and touch

Our sense of touch, or feeling, is more complicated than it seems. It is not just a single sense that detects physical contact, but a multi-sense that feels many different things.

Skin structure

Touch is based in the skin, where there are millions of sensors. As the sensors change size or shape, as a result of being squashed, vibrated, or expanded by heat, they produce nerve signals which are sent to the somatosensory cortex in the brain (see page 180).

In the skin

The largest touch sensors are called Pacinian endings. They have many layers like tiny onions and they are 0.5 millimetres across. The smallest sensors are 100 times tinier than the Pacinian endings. All of these different nerve endings combine to detect the wide range of sensations, including differences in heat and cold, light and heavy touches, vibrations and pain (see page 17).

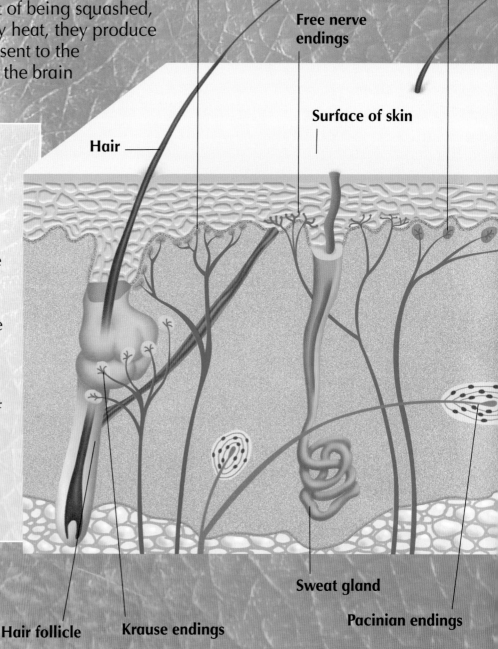

Merkel endings

Meissner endings

Free nerve endings

Surface of skin

Hair

Hair follicle

Krause endings

Sweat gland

Pacinian endings

Scratching

When you feel an itch, your first impulse is to scratch it. Scratching is an important defence mechanism to protect the skin. The itch could be caused by a tick trying to burrow into your skin, and the scratching will knock the tiny creature off before it can dig in.

A magnified image of a tick

Top Facts

- The most touch-sensitive areas of skin include the lips and fingertips. Skin on the fingertips has more than 3000 touch sensors per square centimetre.

- The least sensitive areas are the small of the back and the outer thighs.

- The tongue has touch sensors that tell us about the texture of food.

A cross-section through the skin. The touch sensors (all called 'endings') are mostly in the top 2 millimetres of skin.

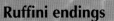

Ruffini endings

Tickling

No one knows why tickling makes us laugh, but this reaction depends greatly on our mood. If we are happy, we laugh when tickled. If we are worried or sad, then tickling can irritate and upset us.

The feet are very sensitive to tickling.

Senses in the brain

The main sensing parts of the body – the eyes, ears, nose, tongue and skin – send nerve signals to the brain. It is only in the brain that we become aware of what we see, hear, smell, taste and touch.

Sense centres

The part of the brain that deals with nerve signals from the skin is called the somatosensory, or touch, centre. This is located on the outer layer of the brain – the cerebral cortex. Different body parts send signals to different parts of this centre. The more sensitive the skin, the larger the cortex area that receives its signals.

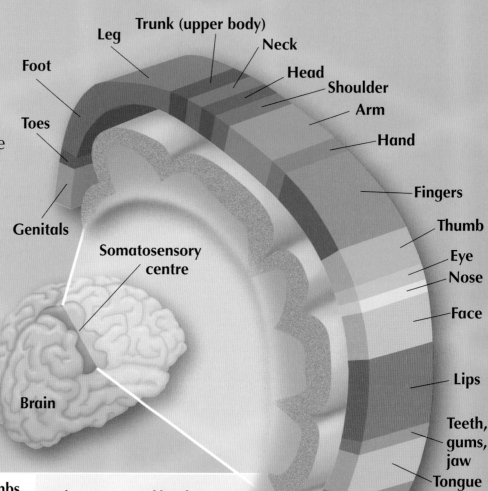

Leg
Trunk (upper body)
Neck
Foot
Head
Shoulder
Arm
Toes
Hand
Fingers
Thumb
Genitals
Eye
Somatosensory centre
Nose
Face
Brain
Lips
Teeth, gums, jaw
Tongue
Pharynx
Intestines

A brain map showing where the different sensory centres for the parts of the body are located and how big they are.

People with amputated limbs, like this walker, may still feel pain in the missing limbs.

Phantom limbs

Sometimes a limb is so badly damaged that it has to be amputated, or removed. The nerves are cut, but the nerve endings often still make signals. The brain may interpret these as coming from the missing limb.

Going upside down on a roller coaster is scary because your senses are confused.

Sense overload

A theme-park ride overwhelms the senses with new sights, feelings and experiences. The senses are thrown into chaos as they try to cope with the body being flung from side to side and upside down.

Putting it together

Like touch, each of the senses has a centre on the cortex (see page 146). These centres constantly communicate with each other by sending nerve signals between themselves. There are also areas that add together the sensory information coming into the brain. These areas give a more complete picture, combining sights, sounds, smells and other senses to form the memory of an experience.

It's Amazing!

Some people have a condition called synaesthesia in which the senses are mixed up. They hear colours, feel sights and smell tastes!

Brain history

In 1808, German scientist Franz Joseph Gall was the first to suggest that different parts of the brain deal with different senses. In the 20th century, Canadian Wilder Penfield and American Theodore Rasmussen worked out a sensory map of the brain.

Soothing sense

Senses can greatly affect our mood. If the skin feels something rough, it puts us on edge. But stroking something soft and warm, such as a pet, creates nerve signals that can have a soothing effect.

Stroking a cat can make you feel happy.

Inner senses

The body has many more senses than just the five main ones. Inside the body, there are microscopic sensors that detect blood content, temperature, the position of the joints and many other things.

Stretch and strain

Muscles have tiny stretch sensors in them that respond to changes in length and to the amount of tension they are under. These sensors are called neuromuscular spindles. They tell the brain the position of the body and limbs, so that we know this information without having to look. This sense is known as proprioceptive or positional sense.

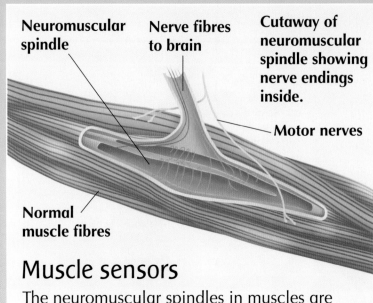

Neuromuscular spindle

Nerve fibres to brain

Cutaway of neuromuscular spindle showing nerve endings inside.

Motor nerves

Normal muscle fibres

Muscle sensors

The neuromuscular spindles in muscles are made up of specialized muscle fibres. These fibres have nerve endings wrapped around them that send information to the brain.

This man is using his positional sense as he practises yoga.

It's Amazing!

Using the body's positional sense, some complicated movements become almost automatic. Many people can tie their shoelaces without looking, even when talking at the same time!

Finger touch test

- In a safe place, close your eyes and hold your hands out in front of you.
- Point the index finger of each hand and slowly move your hands so that the tips of your fingers touch.
- You should be able to do this without looking by using your positional sense.

A boy drinks water because his senses have detected that his body needs water.

Chemical sensors

Sensors in the brain and main blood vessels monitor the levels of certain substances in the blood. These include oxygen, carbon dioxide and glucose (sugar). If carbon dioxide rises and oxygen falls, the brain tells the lungs to breathe faster and deeper. These actions will take in extra oxygen and remove more carbon dioxide. This type of response happens automatically as part of the autonomic nervous system (see page 157).

Fluid levels

If the monitoring sensors in your body report that the levels of some chemicals, such as salts, in your blood are rising, it means the amount of water in your blood has become too low. To deal with this problem, the brain's hypothalamus makes you feel thirsty and want to have a drink.

Body thermostat

The main sensors for body temperature are in the hypothalamus. These sensors monitor the temperature of blood as it flows from the heart to the brain. If the temperature rises, the hypothalamus triggers various reactions to lower it. These include flushed skin, flattened skin hairs and sweating (see page 19).

Sweating is just one of the methods the body uses to maintain body temperature.

Staying balanced

Balance is sometimes called the sixth sense, but it is not really a single sense. It is a continual process of receiving information from several senses and then adjusting the body's muscles to stay steady and not fall over.

Ears and balance

Some information about balance comes from the inner ears. Each inner ear contains semicircular canals and two chambers – the utricle and saccule. The utricle and saccule monitor the position of the head by detecting which way is up, then send nerve signals to the brain.

A gymnast balances on a narrow wooden beam.

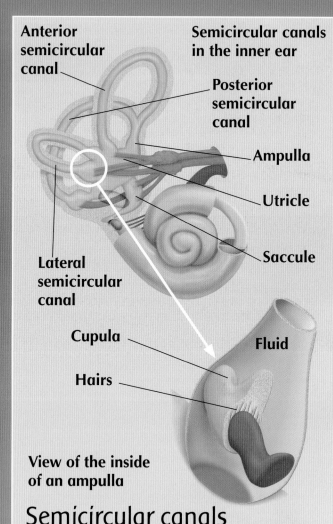

Anterior semicircular canal

Semicircular canals in the inner ear

Posterior semicircular canal

Ampulla

Utricle

Saccule

Lateral semicircular canal

Cupula

Fluid

Hairs

View of the inside of an ampulla

Semicircular canals

At one end of each fluid-filled canal is a pouch called the ampulla. This contains a jelly-like blob, the cupula, which has micro-hairs from hair cells sticking into it. As the head turns, the fluid moves the cupula and the micro-hairs. The hair cells then send signals to the brain.

Unsteady surroundings

In a boat on rough seas, the body is thrown about in an unnatural way. The brain has problems putting together the strange information coming from the inner ears, eyes, skin, muscles and other sensing parts. This can cause feelings of dizziness, nausea and even vomiting, which is called motion or seasickness.

Many people who travel in boats or on ferries get seasick. They can take special pills that help to make them feel better.

More balance input

Information about balance also comes from the eyes. They can see whether the body is the right-way up. Information is also sent by the muscles and joints about the limb positions (see page 182). The brain puts together all this information and then controls various muscles to keep the body in balance.

An astronaut floats weightlessly on the robot arm of the space shuttle.

Balancing test

- In a safe place, stand upright with your arms at your sides and close your eyes. Without the information from your eyes, you may feel unsteady.
- Now, stand on one leg. This makes you even less able to balance. Warning: Open your eyes if you feel you might fall over.

No weight

In space, where there is no gravity, the brain does not receive normal information from the inner ears about which way is up. This can lead to feelings of sickness, dizziness, confusion and headaches. These feelings, known as SAS (Space Adaptation Syndrome), or space sickness, usually pass after a few days.

Eye and ear problems

Any problems that affect the eyes and ears also affect our ability to communicate with other people. New technologies, such as laser eye surgery and electronic hearing aids, help many people to overcome these difficulties.

A group of children learning to communicate using sign language.

It's Amazing!
A horse can hear sounds that are five times quieter than the human ear can detect.

Sign language

People who cannot hear from a young age are unable to listen to others speaking or to the sound of their own voice. This means that they will have problems learning to speak. Sign language allows people who cannot hear to communicate using their fingers and hands – as well as their arms, bodies and facial expressions. These 'signs' combine to represent various words and phrases.

Most hearing aids fit into the ear and are hardly noticeable.

Hearing aids

People who can't hear well, especially if their problem is caused by old age, often wear hearing aids. These change the sound waves into electrical signals and play them back as louder sound waves into the ears.

Sight problems

Common sight problems include cataracts (see page 169) and glaucoma. In glaucoma, the pressure of fluid inside the eye rises and squeezes the retina and nerve fibres. Drugs and surgery are the main treatments for both of these conditions.

Short and long sight

Short sight is when the eyeball is too long, and the lens focuses images of distant objects in front of the retina. This means only near objects can be seen clearly. Long sight is the opposite – the eyeball is too short, meaning that images of near objects are focused behind the retina, so only distant objects are seen clearly.

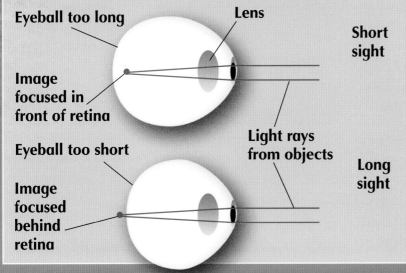

Eyeball too long

Lens

Short sight

Image focused in front of retina

Eyeball too short

Light rays from objects

Long sight

Image focused behind retina

Top Facts

- Cataracts are the most common cause of blindness.

- The most common hearing problems are caused by infections – when germs multiply in the ear. In 'glue ear', the infection causes a sticky fluid that stops the ear bones from vibrating.

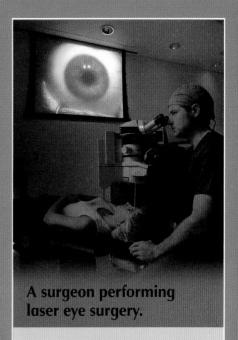

A surgeon performing laser eye surgery.

Eye surgery

Some eye surgery is done with lasers. These shave away parts of the lens or cornea so that rays of light are bent correctly and images focus on the retina.

Protecting the senses

Just a moment with your eyes closed and your hands over your ears shows you how important seeing and hearing are. It is vital to protect these precious senses from damage.

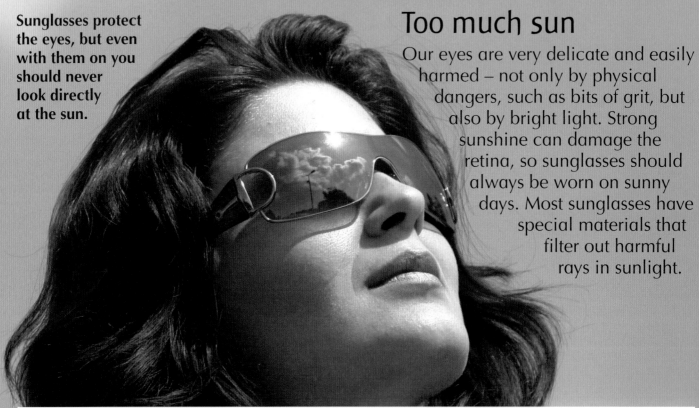

Sunglasses protect the eyes, but even with them on you should never look directly at the sun.

Too much sun

Our eyes are very delicate and easily harmed – not only by physical dangers, such as bits of grit, but also by bright light. Strong sunshine can damage the retina, so sunglasses should always be worn on sunny days. Most sunglasses have special materials that filter out harmful rays in sunlight.

Correcting eyesight

Short or long sight (see page 187) can usually be corrected by wearing glasses or contact lenses. These curved pieces of clear glass or plastic bend the light rays from an object so that the image is focused correctly on the retina and can be seen clearly.

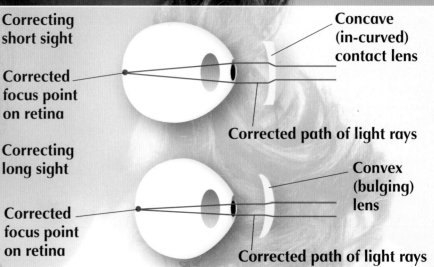

Correcting short sight

Corrected focus point on retina

Concave (in-curved) contact lens

Corrected path of light rays

Correcting long sight

Corrected focus point on retina

Convex (bulging) lens

Corrected path of light rays

Guarding the eyes

People who use welding torches create sparks and flying particles that can damage the eyes. Welders must wear goggles or visors to protect the eyes from the sparks, and also from the brightness of the cutting flame.

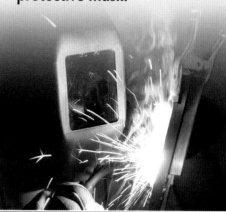

A welder wears a protective mask.

Protecting your hearing

Loud noise that goes on for a long time, especially if it is high-pitched, can gradually affect the hearing. If the delicate nerve endings and hair cells of the cochlea in the ear are damaged by loud noise, it is difficult to repair them. You should avoid listening to music with the volume too high or for too long, especially on your headphones.

Guarding the ears

Ear defenders stop very loud noises from harming the inner ear. They should be worn when using noisy equipment, such as chainsaws, and when working in noisy environments, such as in factories and airports.

A builder wears ear defenders to protect his hearing when cutting stone.

Vision firsts

The first eyeglasses were invented in about 1284 by Salvino D'Armate from Italy. Glass contact lenses were developed in the 1880s, but they were big and heavy. Plastic contact lenses arrived in the 1940s, but the plastic was hard. During the 1950s, soft plastic contact lenses were invented.

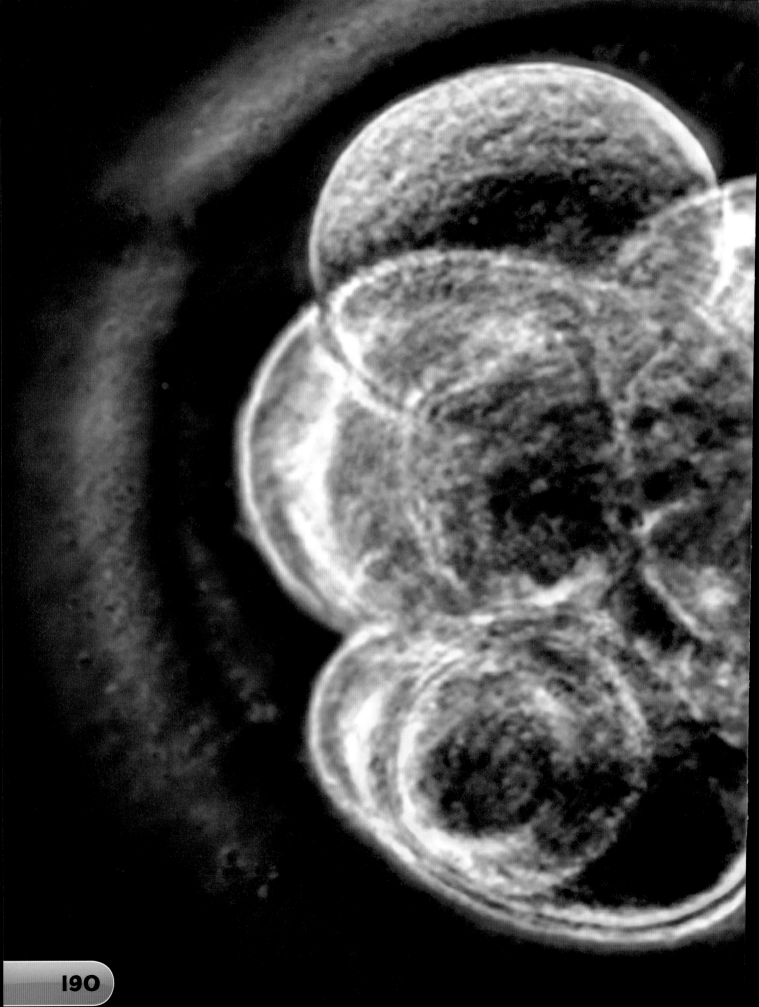

BABIES AND GROWING UP

A baby changes greatly from the day it is a helpless newborn to the day it is a year old – by which time it is probably already walking and starting to talk. Children grow and develop, learning about the world on the way, and eventually become adults. They may then have babies of their own. The parts of the body that make this possible are known as the reproductive system.

Reproductive organs

The parts of the body involved in reproduction are called the reproductive organs, and they differ greatly between men and women. These organs produce the male and female reproductive cells, which need to join. This is called fertilization.

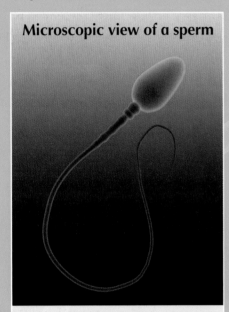

Microscopic view of a sperm

Sperm cells

Each sperm cell has a long tail, which it lashes to swim along. Millions of sperm are produced each day by the testes. They flow out of the testes, through a coiled section of tubes called the epididymis. From here, they pass into long, straight tubes called the ductus deferens. These pass the seminal vesicles and the prostate gland before entering the penis.

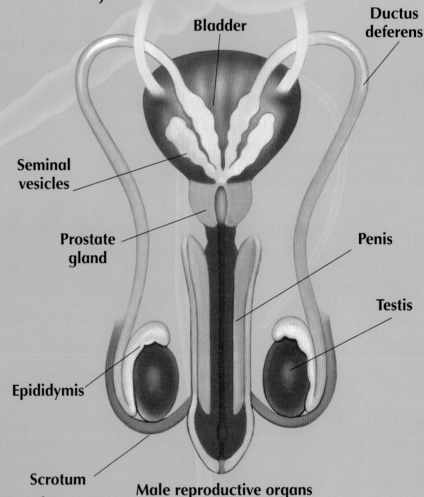

Bladder

Ductus deferens

Seminal vesicles

Prostate gland

Penis

Testis

Epididymis

Scrotum

Male reproductive organs

Male organs

The main male organs are the two testes, or testicles, which make the male reproductive cells – sperm. The testes are found in a skin bag, called the scrotum, which hangs outside the body. While the testes produce the sperm, the seminal vesicles and the prostrate gland produce important liquids that are mixed with the sperm. These liquids provide nutrients and protection for the sperm on their journey to the egg.

Female organs

The main female organs are the two ovaries and the uterus, or womb. The ovaries contain the female reproductive cells – ova, or eggs. In women between the ages of about 11 and 50, the ovaries usually release one egg cell about every four weeks. The egg passes along one of the fallopian tubes towards the womb.

Ovary

Fallopian tube

Womb (uterus)

Ovary

Fallopian tube

Cervix
(neck of the womb)

Birth canal
(vagina)

Female reproductive organs

Sperm first

The first person to see sperm cells was Anton van Leeuwenhoek – a Dutch scientist who made microscopes. In 1677, he drew pictures of the sperm from a man and from a dog and noted how they differed.

It's Amazing!

The reproductive organs are vital for new life, but they are the only system of the body that can be totally removed (perhaps because of disease) without endangering the life of the patient.

Egg release

The egg is one of the largest cells in the body – each measures about 0.1 millimetres across. The release of an egg every month is controlled by hormones (see pages 158–159) in a system called the menstrual cycle. During the menstrual cycle, the lining of the womb thickens – preparing itself to receive a fertilized egg. If the egg is not fertilized (see pages 194–195), the egg leaves the body, along with the lining of the womb, which is no longer needed. This is called menstruating, or a period.

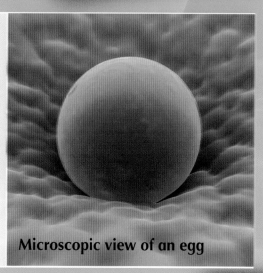

Microscopic view of an egg

New life begins

Sperm are ejaculated into the vagina and then begin their journey to fertilize the egg. Fertilization usually happens in a woman's fallopian tube, when the egg is drifting slowly towards the womb.

Top Facts

- Some sperm reach the fallopian tubes in a few minutes, others take up to 48 hours.

- Fertilization must take place within about 24 hours of an egg being released or the egg will die.

- After fertilization, the egg releases chemicals that stop other sperm from joining with it.

Joining together

Between 300 and 500 million sperm are ejaculated during sexual intercourse, when the man's penis is inside the woman's vagina. The sperm swim into the womb and up the fallopian tubes. Millions of sperm die along the way, and only a few hundred reach the egg. Just one of these may fertilize, or join with, the egg, making it grow into a baby.

A sperm cell burrowing into an egg during fertilization.

Egg division

An egg cell is large, but it divides many times after the sperm fertilizes it. The cells get smaller and smaller until they return to the size of normal body cells. This phase of cell division is called cleavage.

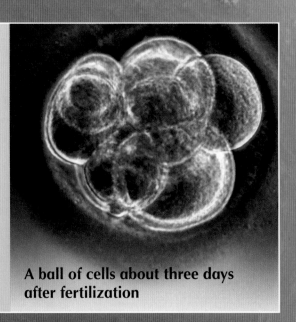

A ball of cells about three days after fertilization

Like all identical twins, these twin sisters look almost exactly alike.

Having twins

Sometimes, two eggs are released by the ovaries and each of them is fertilized by a sperm, resulting in non-identical twins. If a fertilized egg divides into two embryos, the twins are identical. Rarely, there are many embryos – the most to survive is seven.

After fertilization

After fertilization, the single egg cell starts to divide and multiply. After about four or five days, the egg has become a hollow ball of cells called a blastocyst. When this reaches the womb, the ball of cells implants, or sinks, into the womb lining, where it keeps dividing. It is now called an embryo.

It's Amazing!

In the nine months it takes for a baby to develop inside the womb, it increases in size to about 10 billion times the size of the original egg cell.

In vitro fertilization

If a couple cannot have a baby in the usual way, it may be possible for doctors to remove their sperm and eggs and mix them in a dish for fertilization. In some cases, a sperm is injected directly into an egg to fertilize it. The resulting embryo or embryos are put into the womb. Fertilization outside the body is known as 'in vitro fertilization', or IVF. 'In vitro' is Latin for 'in glass'.

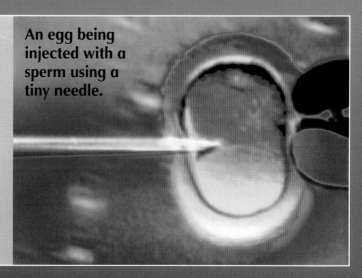

An egg being injected with a sperm using a tiny needle.

Taking shape

The early embryo is a pinhead-size dot that settles into the womb lining. It slowly grows as its cells continue to multiply. About two weeks after fertilization, more changes occur, and a tiny human body starts to form.

This pregnancy test has symbols to show the woman whether or not she is pregnant.

Early embryo

The early embryo forms a flat disc, which will be the body of the baby. The layers of cells on the outside form two protective bags around the baby. The outer protective layer is called the chorion and the inner protective layer is called the amniotic sac. The disc-shaped embryo slowly lengthens, parts of it fold over, and one end becomes a head and the other end a 'tail'. The embryo is fed by a yolk sac and, after about four weeks, by the placenta, which is a spongy mound of tissue inside the womb.

Pregnancy test

As the baby develops, the mother begins to feel different. She can find out whether she is pregnant, or expecting a baby, by testing her urine. A pregnancy test detects a substance called hCG – the levels of which rise during pregnancy.

Animal embryos

Many kinds of animal look alike during the early stages of development. Humans, monkeys, cats, dogs and rabbits all go through similar changes, but they gradually begin to look different. The early human embryo has a tail that shrinks away.

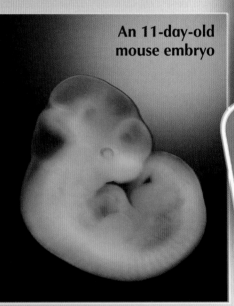

An 11-day-old mouse embryo

It's Amazing!

The heart starts to beat very early in development – less than four weeks after fertilization. At this stage, the embryo is still smaller than a kidney bean.

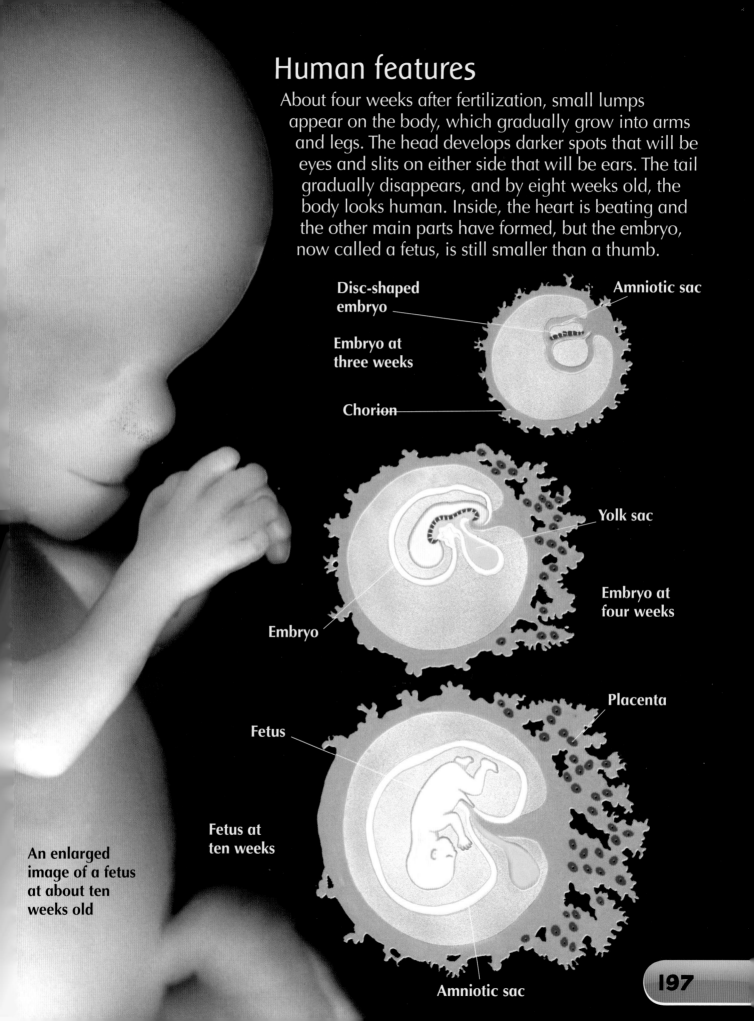

Human features

About four weeks after fertilization, small lumps appear on the body, which gradually grow into arms and legs. The head develops darker spots that will be eyes and slits on either side that will be ears. The tail gradually disappears, and by eight weeks old, the body looks human. Inside, the heart is beating and the other main parts have formed, but the embryo, now called a fetus, is still smaller than a thumb.

Disc-shaped embryo

Amniotic sac

Embryo at three weeks

Chorion

Yolk sac

Embryo

Embryo at four weeks

Placenta

Fetus

Fetus at ten weeks

Amniotic sac

An enlarged image of a fetus at about ten weeks old

197

Growing fast

From eight weeks the fetus grows fast, and soon the mother notices the bulging 'bump' of the baby within her womb.

A nurse checks a pregnant woman's blood pressure.

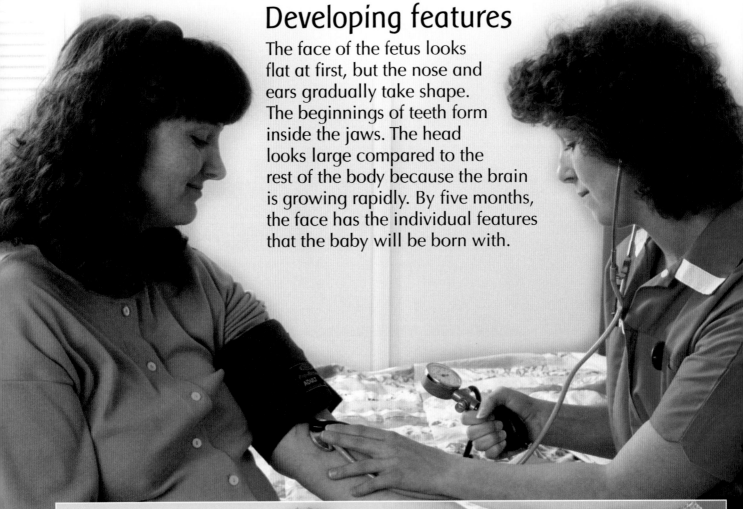

Developing features

The face of the fetus looks flat at first, but the nose and ears gradually take shape. The beginnings of teeth form inside the jaws. The head looks large compared to the rest of the body because the brain is growing rapidly. By five months, the face has the individual features that the baby will be born with.

Amniotic fluid

Umbilical cord

Placenta

Fetus at 20 weeks

Food and shelter

The fetus floats in amniotic fluid, which cushions and protects it. The fetus's blood flows to and from the placenta along a system of blood vessels called the umbilical cord. The placenta passes oxygen and nutrients from the mother's blood to the fetus's blood and takes away waste.

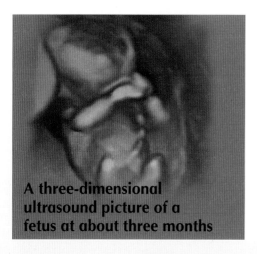

A three-dimensional ultrasound picture of a fetus at about three months

Ultrasound

The fetus's development can be checked by taking pictures inside the womb using an ultrasound machine (see page 90). Most expectant mothers have scans at 10 to 13 and 18 to 20 weeks.

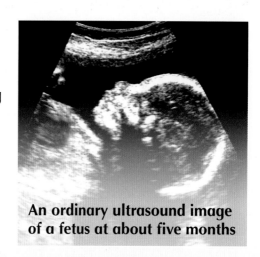

An ordinary ultrasound image of a fetus at about five months

It's Amazing!

The fetus makes movements as it tests its developing muscles. It kicks, punches, turns somersaults and even hiccups and sucks its thumb.

Bigger body

By six months, the body, arms and legs have grown quickly to catch up with the large head. At first, the fingers and toes have webs of skin between them, but these disappear and the nails grow. A covering of fine hair, called lanugo, develops on the skin, but it usually falls away before birth.

Top Facts

- At six months, the fetus looks slim and has wrinkled skin.

- At seven months, the fetus begins to put on fat under the skin.

- By eight months, the fetus has a chubby appearance.

- At nine months, the fetus is fully developed and ready to be born.

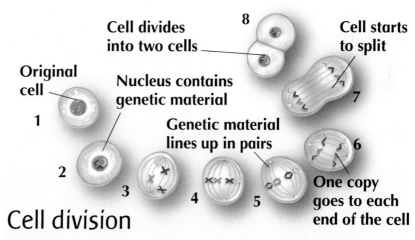

Cell divides into two cells

Cell starts to split

Original cell

Nucleus contains genetic material

Genetic material lines up in pairs

One copy goes to each end of the cell

Cell division

The fetus's body grows as cells divide and multiply in their millions inside it. Each cell contains genes, or a set of instructions, that tell the cell what to do (see pages 214–215). As it divides, the cell copies its genetic material, and one copy goes to each end of the cell. The cell then splits in the middle to produce two offspring cells. This sequence of cell division happens billions of times as the fetus develops inside the womb.

Birth day

About 266 days after the baby started to develop from a fertilized egg, the mother feels her womb muscles tightening. Slowly, the baby is squeezed from the womb along the birth canal (vagina) to the outside world.

It's Amazing!
More babies are born between 3 and 4 am than at any other hour. But fewer are born between 3 and 4 pm than at any other hour.

A tiring day

The process of giving birth is sometimes called labour. It takes a huge amount of effort and is very tiring for both mother and baby. It may take more than 24 hours, especially for a mother having her first baby, and can be painful. Babies are usually born head-first, but some are born feet-first, while others are delivered by surgery in an operation called a Caesarean section.

Just before labour, most fetuses move into a head-down position, ready for birth.

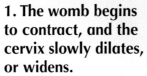

The baby drops lower in the pelvis.

1. The womb begins to contract, and the cervix slowly dilates, or widens.

2. The contractions push the baby's head through the cervix into the birth canal.

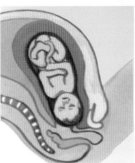

3. The head emerges first from the mother, and the rest of the body soon follows.

Giving birth

During birth, the womb muscles contract and then relax. As labour progresses, the contractions become stronger and more frequent, slowly pushing the baby out of the womb. The placenta is pushed out about 30 minutes after the baby is born.

Checks at birth

After the birth, the new baby's colour, breathing, heartbeat and eyes are all examined. The arms and legs are moved to check the muscles and joints. The fingers and toes are counted.

After examining and cleaning the baby, the doctor or nurse cuts the umbilical cord.

Cry baby

When the baby is delivered, it is still attached to the placenta by the umbilical cord. The doctors or midwives then cut the umbilical cord and encourage the baby to cry. This helps the baby's lungs to open and take its first breaths of air. The baby may then take its first feed of milk from its mother's breast.

A baby just after it has been born.

Some premature babies go into special cots called incubators to keep them warm.

Premature baby

If a baby is born more than three weeks early, it is premature. These babies may not have had time to develop properly and may need special care.

Top Facts

- Worldwide, more boys are born than girls – about 105 to 106 boys for every 100 girls.

- The average pregnancy for girls is one day longer than the pregnancy for boys.

- The most common month for births is August and the least common is April.

First weeks

A new baby is fairly helpless and does little except feed, sleep and cry. Within a few weeks, changes start to happen, and the baby begins to learn to do more things.

Muscles and moving

A newborn baby's muscles are not very strong and do not work together well. Gradually, the baby learns to move its neck, body, arms and legs. It makes test movements, feels and watches the results and tries again. By this trial-and-error method, its movements become more purposeful and better controlled.

A breast-feeding baby. Breast-feeding makes babies feel comforted and secure as they snuggle up to their mothers.

Smiling is a good way for a baby to get attention.

Smiling

Most babies smile in the first four to six weeks. At first, the baby may simply be trying out different face muscles. But after a while, the child notices that smiling gets a positive response, such as a sound or a smile, and so smiles more.

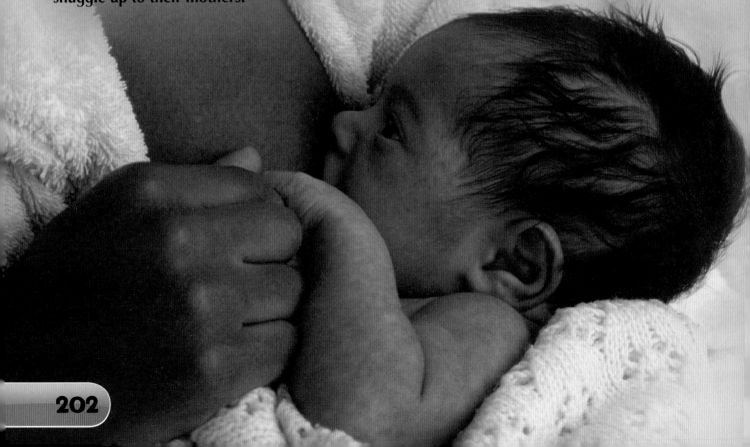

Feeding

Just before birth, a mother starts to produce milk through her breasts. At first, mother's breast milk contains all the baby needs to grow. After about six months, most babies move on to solid foods – this is called weaning.

A baby being fed a meal of pureed food.

Developing senses

A new baby's senses of sight and hearing are not very well developed just after birth. At first, the child cannot understand the jumble of sounds around it. After a time, it begins to link certain noises, such as its mother's voice, with feelings of warmth and comfort. The eyes also become able to focus properly, so that the baby can see both nearby and distant things clearly.

It's Amazing!

Many babies are born with blue eyes that later change colour. The eye colour, determined by a substance called pigment, may not develop properly for several months.

Be a baby!

- Try being a baby for a few minutes. Close your eyes and feel one hand with the other hand. Hold your hands out and try to touch your thumbs together.
- Before new babies can see things clearly, they use their sense of touch to explore the world around them.

Some babies chew on teething rings.

Teething

A baby's first teeth start to come through after about six months, and the gums may become red and sore. The baby may dribble more and chew toys and other items. Doing this seems to relieve some of the discomfort the new teeth are causing.

Learning fast

A young child learns very quickly. Crawling and walking are soon mastered. There may be some bumps and falls, but these are soon forgotten because the world is a very exciting place.

New skills

One skill that babies soon learn is hand-to-eye co-ordination. This involves watching with the eyes as the hands pick up objects, such as toys and cups. At about nine months, most babies can crawl on all fours. They also learn to pull themselves up into a standing position. By about 18 months, most babies can walk on their own.

Drawing the wrong way

- Draw a smiley face with a pencil. Now, hold the pencil in your 'other' hand. If you are right handed, this will be your left hand.
- Try to draw the same face with the 'wrong' hand. It takes much more time and effort. If you practise, you gradually improve. This is how young children learn, by trying and practising.

As this baby crawls, her arms and legs quickly become stronger.

Social skills

Learning is not only about movement and physical skills. A young child must also learn about other people. He or she will learn how to communicate and make friends with other children. Sharing toys and taking turns teaches young children that other people matter, and that they may not always get their own way.

It's Amazing!

Most healthy babies weigh between 3-4 kilograms at birth. By five months, their weight has doubled, and by their first birthday, they weigh three times as much!

Learning to walk

Walking seems so easy, but if you watch a young child, you will see how difficult it is at first. A young child's head is big, heavy and unsteady compared to its body, limbs and muscle strength. This makes it difficult for the child to balance without falling over.

At first, a baby needs help from an adult to walk.

Development stages

All children learn at different rates, but the table below is a guideline to the things most children can do when they reach a certain age.

Age in months	Skills
0–3	Responds to loud sounds. Notices own hands. Smiles at sound of parent's voice. Supports own head. Reaches for toys.
3–6	Brings hands together. Turns head to sounds. Rolls over from stomach to back and from back to stomach. Can bear some of own weight on legs. Supports some weight on outstretched arms when on stomach.
6–9	Can sit unsupported. Can crawl. Holds a bottle.
9–12	Pulls on things to stand up. Can say at least one word. Can walk holding on to furniture.
12–18	Can hold a cup without spilling. Walks across a room without falling. Walks without support or help. Can say at least two words. Takes off own shoes. Can eat without help.

The growing body

During childhood, the body gets bigger and its muscles become stronger. The brain learns how to control movements so that they become smoother and more skilful.

Size comparison

The rate at which children grow will vary from one child to another. This rate is dependent upon many things, such as diet and the amount of certain hormones in the body. Even children who are the same age may vary considerably in height and weight.

Children of different heights and ages

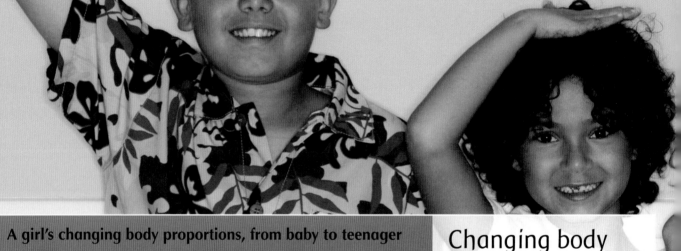

Changing body

As a child grows up, the proportions of different body parts change. A new baby's head is almost a quarter of its height, as are its legs. By adulthood, the head makes up only an eighth of the height while the legs make up about half.

A girl's changing body proportions, from baby to teenager

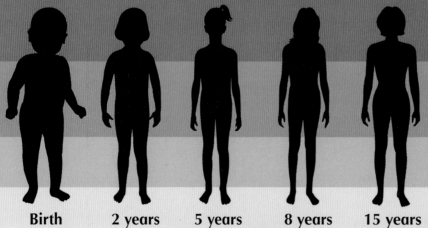

| Birth | 2 years | 5 years | 8 years | 15 years |

Height change

- Due to better nutrition, people today are taller than ever. About 500 years ago, few adult men were more than 1.55 metres tall.
- The average height today in a country such as the USA is about 1.60 to 1.65 metres for women and 1.75 to 1.80 metres for men.

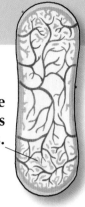

Growth plates

Growth plate hardens and seals.

New bone

Cross-sections of growing bones

Longer bones

Most of the body's height comes from the long bones in the legs. These grow from sites called the growth plates near each end of the bone. These areas make bone tissue that is added to the middle of the bone, making it longer. The growth plates close up when children reach their full adult height.

How growth happens

Growth is largely controlled by a substance called growth hormone (see pages 158–159), which is made in an area under the front of the brain called the pituitary gland. Growth hormone travels around in the blood and encourages cells to multiply and body parts to grow. Some people naturally have slightly less or more growth hormone, which is one of the reasons why we vary in size. If this causes a problem, it can be treated by an operation or injections.

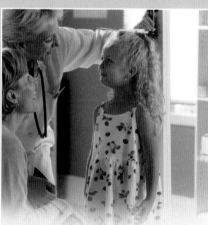

A doctor measures this girl's height as part of a checkup.

Growing up

It's fun to record your height and weight, perhaps on your birthday each year. You may notice that your growth rate varies. Babies grow quickly up until about three years old, then the rate slows until they reach the teenage years.

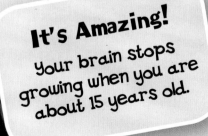

It's Amazing!
Your brain stops growing when you are about 15 years old.

Children taking part in a school sports day.

Off to school

At school, children are educated, which means they are taught all sorts of information that will be useful to them in later life.

Learning in school

At first, children learn basic skills, such as reading, writing and simple maths. As children get older, the lessons gradually get harder, and the range of subjects increases.

Making decisions

Physical activity, including taking part in sports or games, is vital for children. It teaches children about taking risks and making decisions in a safe environment.

Children learning to swim.

Healthy body

Skills that involve movement are called motor skills. Taking part in physical activities, such as swimming, improves a child's motor skills. It also exercises their muscles and strengthens their bones.

Other kinds of learning

At school, children mix in larger groups than they have done before. As a result, they have to learn more advanced social skills, such as how to be polite and make friends. These friends may then influence many of their likes and dislikes, such as food, clothes, games and music. Children also learn to work with others as a team.

This teacher asks her pupils a lot of questions to test their knowledge and encourage them to take part.

Memory experiment

- Some of our strongest memories are probably 'firsts'. Can you recall your first day at school? Everything may have seemed strange, and you were probably nervous.
- Think back to some other 'firsts'. For example, the first time you saw a baby brother or sister. Can you remember 'seconds'? That's much less likely!

It's Amazing!

As children listen, talk, read and write, they learn an average of more than ten words every day. Which new words have you learned recently?

New skills

Abilities based on thinking rather than doing, such as reading, are called mental skills. Playing a musical instrument combines both mental and motor skills.

Playing an instrument, such as this violin, gets easier with practice.

The teen years

Just before and during the teenage years, the body changes rapidly. This time of transition from childhood to adulthood is called adolescence.

Puberty

The physical changes that happen at this time are called puberty. Girls start to make a hormone called oestrogen, and boys make testosterone. Oestrogen causes a girl's ovaries to release eggs, and she starts to menstruate once a month (see page 193). Testosterone makes a boy's testes produce sperm (see page 192).

Top Facts

- On average, girls begin puberty at 10 to 11 years and boys at 12 to 13.

- The changes happen faster in girls, and are usually complete by the age of 15.

- In boys, the changes take longer and growth continues until the age of 18.

Hormonal changes during adolescence mean that teenagers look to become more independent and they may take part in risky activities, such as snowboarding.

Skin problems

A common problem for teenagers is acne. The hormonal changes that take place at this age cause the skin to make more sebum, which gets trapped in the skin pores and causes acne (see page 30). Bad acne can be treated with special creams or drugs prescribed by a doctor.

Acne on the face may make a teenager feel embarrassed and self-conscious.

Social changes

As teenagers get older, they become more independent. They spend less time with their family and more time with people of their own age. This is a time of emotional changes, and relationships with parents can become strained. The rise in hormones makes adolescents more interested in the opposite sex.

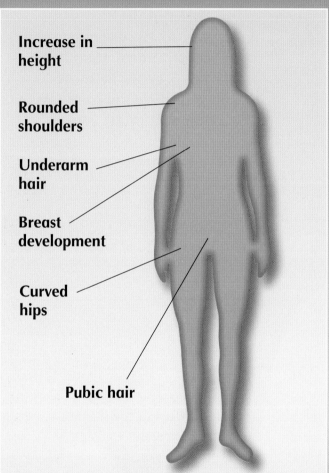

Increase in height

Rounded shoulders

Underarm hair

Breast development

Curved hips

Pubic hair

Female changes

During puberty, the female body grows in height rapidly. The breasts get larger, and the body outline becomes more curved, with pads of fat on the hips. Hair grows under the armpits, and also between the legs. Also, the voice deepens slightly.

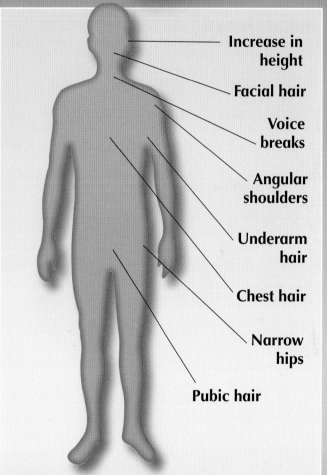

Increase in height

Facial hair

Voice breaks

Angular shoulders

Underarm hair

Chest hair

Narrow hips

Pubic hair

Male changes

During puberty, a boy's body grows in height even more rapidly than a girl's. The body outline becomes more angular, with wide shoulders. Hair grows on the face, on the chest, under the armpits and between the legs. A boy's voice deepens, or breaks, much more than a girl's does.

Maturing

Most people are fully grown by 20 years old, but their muscles continue to develop for another 10 years. By 40 to 50 years, some body systems start to show signs of ageing.

Adulthood

As people reach adulthood, many of them form a close relationship with another adult and start a family. While men can produce sperm and father children throughout their life, women will stop releasing eggs at about the age of 50. This is called the menopause.

Life expectancy

The human body's average lifespan has increased through the centuries due to improved healthcare. About 500 years ago, living beyond the age of 50 years was unusual. In most wealthy countries today, many men live to 75 years or more and many women pass the age of 80 years.

A family enjoys a picnic.

The ageing body

As people age, the number of cells in their body reduces because cells die and some are not replaced. This means that some systems in the body do not work as well. This graph shows how things, such as mental ability (brain weight), making energy from food (metabolism), circulation (resting heart rate) and breathing (lung capacity) do not function as well after the age of 25.

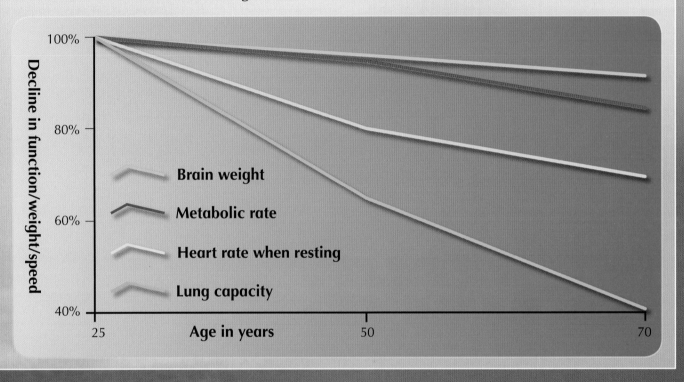

Decline in function/weight/speed

- Brain weight
- Metabolic rate
- Heart rate when resting
- Lung capacity

100%
80%
60%
40%

25   Age in years   50   70

Ageing

Signs of ageing include grey hair, wrinkled skin, difficulty moving and memory loss. The age at which people show these signs varies. This is partly due to their genes (see pages 214–215) and partly due to their lifestyle. Not smoking and eating a healthy diet helps people look younger for longer.

This old man keeps fit by going for a walk in the park.

Old age

Although people can retire in their 60s, some keep working because they enjoy it. Even after retiring, many people start new hobbies and make new friendships. By keeping active, both physically and mentally, people can enjoy many healthy years in old age.

Genes and heredity

Everything in the human body is organized by a set of instructions called genes, which are found in a chemical called DNA.

The genome

The genome is the full set of instructions for the growth, development, maintenance and repair of the human body. It consists of an estimated 25,000 to 27,000 different genes. These genes lie in every single cell where they are found in a long, chemical code, called DNA (see below). The DNA is twisted into X-shaped objects called chromosomes. The genes control everything about you, including eye colour, skin colour, hair type and ear shape.

DNA molecule

DNA ladder

Deoxyribonucleic acid, or DNA, is shaped like a ladder twisted into a corkscrew called a double helix. The 'rungs' of this ladder shape are chemicals called bases. There are four kinds: adenine (A), thymine (T), guanine (G) and cytosine (C). These bases are joined in pairs, and a single gene is a section of the DNA molecule that contains hundreds of these base pairs, which are arranged in a specific order.

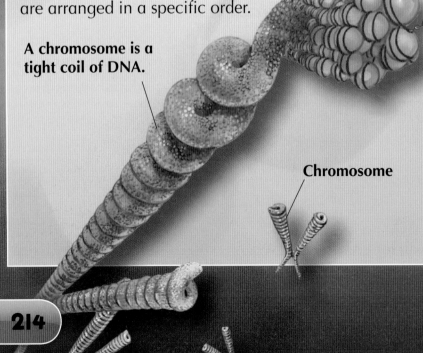

A chromosome is a tight coil of DNA.

Chromosome

Genetic work

The structure of DNA was discovered in 1953 by English scientist Francis Crick and American researcher James Watson. In 2000, the Human Genome Project, which is made up of scientists from all over the world, worked out the entire sequence of DNA bases in human chromosomes.

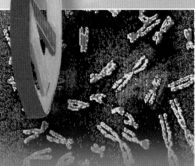

Rungs on the double helix are pairs of the bases guanine, adenine, thymine and cytosine.

Uncoiled image of a DNA molecule showing its double helix shape.

A microscopic image of chromosomes

Chromosomes

Each chromosome is formed from a long bit of DNA, like a twisted piece of string. Every cell in your body has 23 pairs of chromosomes inside it, making a total of 46 chromosomes per cell.

It's Amazing!

If you could straighten all the pieces of DNA in a single cell and join them end to end, they would stretch about 1.5 metres.

Passing on genes

When a cell multiplies, it copies its chromosomes, so that each new cell receives 46 chromosomes. When sperm and egg cells are made, however, each of them contains only 23 chromosomes. When the egg and sperm join, they make a complete set of 46 chromosomes again. The baby has genes from the father and mother and so inherits, or receives, features from them both.

Down's syndrome

Some people have an extra or missing chromosome, rather than the usual 23 pairs. In a condition called Down's syndrome, there are three of chromosome number 21 instead of two, giving them a total of 47 chromosomes. Down's syndrome occurs in about 1 in 800 births.

Two children with Down's syndrome

Adipose tissue
Tissue that contains a lot of fat, including the fat layer under the skin.

Alveoli
The endings of the terminal bronchioles inside the lungs. These are the sites of gas exchange between air in the lungs and the blood.

Antagonistic muscles
Muscles that pull in opposite directions, so that a joint can both extend and shorten.

Aorta
The body's main artery. It carries blood from the left side of the heart to the rest of the body.

Arteries
Blood vessels that carry blood away from the heart. The larger arteries have thick, muscular walls because the blood inside them is at high pressure.

Asthma
A physcial condition where breathing becomes difficult because the airways have constricted. Asthma can be caused by stress, allergies or cold weather.

Atrium
One of the two upper chambers of the heart. The atria are filled with blood that flows into the heart from the veins.

Bacterium
Small, single-celled organism. Some bacteria are helpful to people, helping with, for example, digestion. Others are harmful, and can cause sickness and infections.

Blood plasma
The clear, yellowish liquid that makes up most of the blood in the body.

Bone marrow
Soft, jelly-like substance found inside many bones. The marrow in some bones makes blood cells.

Bronchi
The large airways that branch from the trachea and run to the lungs.

Bronchioles
Small tubes that branch from the bronchi and continue to divide until they reach the terminal bronchioles and alveoli.

Cancellous bone
Also called spongy bone, this is a type of bone tissue that lies inside longer bones, such as the femur. Cancellous bone has many holes that are filled with red bone marrow where blood cells are made.

Canine teeth
Sharp, pointed teeth that are found near the front of the mouth, just behind the incisors.

Capillaries
The tiny blood vessels that link the arteries to the veins.

Cardiac muscle
A type of muscle tissue that is only found in the heart.

Cardiovascular system
The network of blood vessels that, along with the heart, carries blood around the body.

Cartilage
A soft tissue that can support parts of the body, such as the nose, and helps joints, such as the knee, to move smoothly.

Cell
The basic unit of all living things. Inside most cells is a nucleus containing the genetic information about the organism.

Chromosome
A very long strand of DNA that is found inside the nucleus of a cell.

Cilia
Tiny hair-like structures that stick out of some cells and can wave with a rhythmic motion. Cilia are found lining the airways.

Cuticle
The sensitive area around the base of the nail. It is also called the 'quick'.

Dehydration

A condition when the body does not contain enough water. This is due to a person either not drinking enough water or losing too much fluid.

Dermis

The second layer of the skin. The dermis lies just under the epidermis.

Diaphragm

The dome-shaped sheet of muscle that lies beneath the lungs. During breathing, the diaphragm flattens to increase the volume of the lungs and to pull air into them.

Diastolic pressure

The blood pressure between each heart beat. It is the second figure given during a blood pressure reading.

DNA

Short for deoxyribonucleic acid. DNA is arranged in a twin spiral shape, called a double helix, and it contains the genetic instructions for every cell. These instructions are collected together in genes and are inherited from parents.

Echocardiogram

A machine that uses sound waves and their echoes to build up a 'picture' of the heart. A similar machine produces ultrasound images of an unborn baby.

Embolus

An object that travels through the circulatory system and which can cause an embolism, or blockage, in a blood vessel. An embolus can be made from a small blood clot that has broken away.

Epidermis

The topmost layer of skin. Skin cells divide at the base of the epidermis and are pushed up to the surface, flattening and dying as they move upwards.

Epiglottis

A flap of cartilage that drops down to cover the larynx during swallowing. This stops food and drink from entering the airways and choking a person.

Faeces

Waste products left over from the digestive system.

Fibrin

A type of protein that forms long strands during the blood clotting process to trap red blood cells and form a clot.

Fontanelles

Soft areas on a baby's head between the harder skull bones. These soft spots allow the baby's skull to be squashed slightly during birth, to make passage through the cervix easier.

Genes

The biological instructions found inside every human cell. Each gene controls a feature or function of the body. Genes are made up of sections of DNA.

Glands

Collections of cells and tissues that produce substances for release, such as endocrine glands that make hormones.

Hair follicle

A narrow pocket in the skin from which a hair grows.

Haversian system

Concentric rings of bone tissue that make up compact bone.

Hay fever

An allergic reaction to plant pollen. It usually results in a runny nose, streaming eyes and sneezing.

Hormone

A chemical that regulates an amount or the rate of a body process. For example, insulin regulates the amount of sugar in the blood.

Incisor teeth

Chisel-shaped teeth that are found at the front of the mouth. It is their role to chop off pieces of food.

Integumentary system

The skin, hair and nails.

Joint

The point where two or more bones meet. Joints can be rigid, as in the skull, or they can bend, such as those in the wrist, ankle, knee or elbow.

Larynx

The opening to the lower respiratory tract where the vocal cords are located. Also called the voice box.

Ligaments

Thick fibres that run across joints. They link one bone to another and stop the bones from moving too far apart.

Lobe

A large section of an organ. For example, the liver is made up of two lobes.

Lymphocyte

A type of white blood cell that plays an important role in the body's immune system, identifying and destroying potentially dangerous substances, such as bacteria.

Macrophages

Large white blood cells that are involved in phagocytosis when foreign objects, such as bacteria, are engulfed by the cell and destroyed.

Melanin

The skin's natural pigment, or colouring. It is produced by special cells called melanocytes, which lie in the bottom of the epidermis.

Menstrual cycle

The 28-day cycle in which an egg is released from an ovary in an adult woman and the lining of the womb builds up. At the end of the cycle, if the egg is not fertilized, the egg and the womb lining are released during menstruation.

Microscope

A device for looking cloesly at objects. Optical microscopes use lenses to make objects appear larger.

Molar teeth

Large flattened teeth that are found near the rear of the mouth. With the premolars, it is their role to crush and chew food.

Muscle fibres

A collection of muscle cells that have a long, tube-like shape. They can contract to make a muscle shorter and pull on a bone.

Oesophagus

The tube that leads down from the throat and into the stomach. Also called the gullet.

Ovaries

The female reproductive organs. Each ovary contains hundreds of eggs and, usually, a single egg is released every 28 days.

Peristalsis

The wave-like movements in a tube that are caused by contractions of the smooth muscle in its wall. These push the tube's contents along.

Perspiration

Water produced by sweat glands in the skin that helps to keep the body cool. It is also called sweat.

Pharynx

A tube leading from the back of the nasal passages and the mouth to the larynx and oesophagus. It is also called the throat.

Platelet

A type of blood cell. Platelets are important in forming blood clots to heal any cuts and leaks.

Premolar teeth

Flattened teeth that lie between the canine teeth and the molars. Their role is to crush and chew food.

Pus

A thick yellow liquid that is produced during an infection. It is made up of white blood cells, the remains of body cells and foreign organisms, such as bacteria.

Rugae

Folds found on the lining of the stomach. They allow the stomach to expand when food is swallowed.

Sebaceous gland

A small gland that is usually found next to a hair follicle. Sebaceous glands produce the skin oil called sebum.

Serum

Part of the blood plasma that is left behind after blood clotting has occurred.

Sinus

A cavity inside a body organ or tissue. For example, the front of the skull contains a number of sinuses, which are called the paranasal sinuses.

Smooth muscle

A type of muscle tissue that acts automatically. When looked at under a microscope, it looks smooth and lacks the bands of striated muscle fibres.

Sphygmomanometer

A machine that is used to measure blood pressure.

Striated muscle

A type of muscle tissue that moves the bones of the skeleton. Under a microscope, this muscle tissue appears to have bands, or striations, hence its name.

Synovial fluid

The thick fluid found inside cavities in some joints, such as the knee. Synovial fluid acts as a lubricant in these joints.

Systolic pressure

The blood pressure when the heart pushes blood out into the arteries. It is the first figure given in a blood pressure reading.

Tendon

Thick fibres that attach muscles to the bones. The muscles pull on the tendons which, in turn, pull on the bones to create a movement.

Testes

The male sex organs. The testes produce sperm and they hang outside the body, inside a sac called the scrotum.

Trachea

The tube that leads from the larynx down into the chest and branches to form the bronchi. It is also called the windpipe.

Uvula

A soft, muscular flap that hangs from the soft palate at the back of the mouth. It is used to make some sounds during speech and vibrates loudly during snoring.

Veins

Blood vessels that carry blood back to the heart, usually under low pressure. The larger veins have valves inside them to stop blood from flowing the wrong way.

Ventricle

One of the two lower chambers of the heart. The thick, muscular walls of the ventricles contract to push blood out of the heart and into the arteries leading to the lungs and the rest of the body.

Vertebrae

The name of the bones that make up the spine, or backbone. They protect the spinal cord.

Villi

Tiny, finger-like projections that stick out from the lining of the intestine. They increase the surface area of the intestine, making it easier for the body to absorb nutrients.

Water vapour

Water in its gas state.

WEBLINKS

http://www.bbc.co.uk/science/humanbody/

http://www.bbc.co.uk/health/index.shtml

http://www.learnenglish.org.uk/kids/archive/theme_body.html

http://yucky.discovery.com/noflash/body/

http://www.kidshealth.org/kid/

http://nobelprize.org/educational_games/medicine/

http://www.medtropolis.com/VBody.asp

http://www.brainpop.com/health/

http://www.kidskonnect.com/HumanBody/HumanBody.html

http://www.healthfinder.gov/kids/

http://www.lung.ca/children/index_kids.html

http://www.bam.gov/

INDEX

ACKNOWLEDGEMENTS

Artwork supplied through the Art Agency by Terry Pastor, Barry Croucher,
Robin Carter and Dave Smith

Photo credits:
b = bottom, t = top, r = right, l = left, c = center

Front cover c Micro Discovery/Corbis, tl Don Mason/Corbis, tc Simon Jaratt/Corbis, tr Tom Grill/Corbis, bl Lester Lefkowitz/Corbis, br Mehaykulyk/Science Photo Library
Back cover br Anette Linnea Rasmussen/Dreamstime.com, tr Germán Ariel Berra/Dreamstime.com, bl Digital Art/Corbis, bc Jens Nieth/Corbis

1 Dreamstime.com, 2-3 William Attard Mccarthy/Dreamstime.com, 3c Dreamstime.com, 4-5 75 Zena Holloway/zefa/Corbis, 8-9 Micro Discovery/Corbis, 10-11 William Attard Mccarthy/Dreamstime.com, 10cl Anette Linnea Rasmussen/Dreamstime.com, 10cr Dreamstime.com, 11tl Pierre Lahalle/TempSport/Corbis, 12-13 Visuals Unlimited/Corbis, 13tr Ljupco Smokovski/Dreamstime.com, 14-15 Gabe Palmer/zefa/Corbis, 14l Dreamstime.com, 15tr Dreamstime.com, 16-17 Lawrence Manning/CORBIS, 16tr Dreamstime.com, 18-19 Fritz Langmann/Dreamstime.com, 19tr S. Carmona/CORBIS, 20-21 Visuals Unlimited/Corbis, 21tr Reuters/CORBIS, 22-23 Dreamstime.com, 22bl Karen Struthers/Dreamstime.com, 23tr Dreamstime.com, 23bl Jonathan Pais/ Dreamstime.com, 24-25 Anthony Redpath/CORBIS, 25tr Mediscan/Corbis, 25bl Dreamstime.com, 26-27 Fendis/zefa/Corbis, 27tr Visuals Unlimited/Corbis, 27bl Anke Van Wyk/Dreamstime.com, 28-29 Susanne Dittrich/zefa/Corbis, 28cl Anna Moller/zefa/Corbis, 29br Jaimie Duplass/Dreamstime.com, 30-31 Lester V. Bergman/CORBIS, 31br Wendy Kaveney/Dreamstime.com, 32-33 Grace/zefa/Corbis, 32c Visuals Unlimited/Corbis, 33tr Rob Marmion/Dreamstime.com, 33bl Carolina k. Smith m.d./ Dreamstime.com, 34-35 Visuals Unlimited/Corbis, 36tc Dreamstime.com, 37bl Bettmann/CORBIS, 38-39 and 39bl Lester V. Bergman/CORBIS, 38cl Lester V. Bergman/CORBIS, 40-41 Geir-olav Lyngfjell/Dreamstime.com, 41tl Dreamstime.com, 41bc Manuela Krause/Dreamstime.com, 42-43 Duomo/CORBIS, 42bl all Dreamstime.com, 43cr Dreamstime.com, 43bc Dreamstime.com, 44-45 Lester V. Bergman/CORBIS, 44cr Dreamstime.com, 45br Lester V. Bergman/CORBIS, 46-47 Linda Bucklin/Dreamstime.com, 46 Janet Carr/Dreamstime. com, 47tc Oleg Kozlov/Dreamstime.com, 47cr Rod Ferris/Dreamstime.com, 48-49 and 48br Ron Boardman; Frank Lane Picture Agency/CORBIS, 49tr Sue Colvil/Dreamstime.com, 49cl Dreamstime.com, 50-51 Sean Nel/Dreamstime.com, 51tr Dreamstime.com, 51br Anton Novozhilov/Dreamstime.com, 52-53 Linda Bucklin/Dreamstime.com, 52bl Dreamstime. com, 53tr Jurie Maree/Dreamstime.com, 55br Dreamstime.com, 56-57 Eddy Lemaistre/Photo & Co./Corbis, 57tl Dreamstime.com - Marek Tihelka, 57cl Dreamstime.com, 58-59 Michael DeYoung/Corbis, 58cl Lester V. Bergman/CORBIS, 59cr Anneke Schram/Dreamstime.com, 60-61 Ben Welsh/zefa/Corbis, 62cl Graça Victoria/Dreamstime.com, 62br Dreamstime.com, 63tr Jaimie Duplass/Dreamstime.com, 63b Katrina Brown/Dreamstime.com, 64-65 Dreamstime.com, 65tr Pete Saloutos/zefa/Corbis, 65br David Badenhorst/Dreamstime.com, 66-67 Najlah Feanny/Corbis, 67tr Lester V. Bergman/CORBIS, 68-69 Robbie Jack/Corbis, 69c Howard Sandler Dreamstime.com, 70-71 Lester V. Bergman/CORBIS, 71br Mediscan/Corbis, 72-73 Visuals Unlimited/Corbis, 73tr Lester V. Bergman/CORBIS, 74-75 Zena Holloway/zefa/Corbis, 75cr Daniel Gale/Dreamstime.com, 75bl Anthony J. Hall/Dreamstime.com, 77tr Sonya Etchison/Dreamstime.com, 77br Roman Milert/Dreamstime.com, 78-79 Awilli/zefa/Corbis, 79cl John Sartin/Dreamstime.com, 79tr Randy Faris/Corbis, 80-81 Stephen Sweet/ Dreamstime.com, 81cr Mediscan/Corbis, 81br Will Moneymaker/Dreamstime.com, 82-83 Karen Kasmauski/CORBIS, 82bc Micro Discovery/Corbis, 83cr Peter Elvidge/Dreamstime.com, 83bc Bob Sacha/Corbis, 84-85 tienne Poupinet/zefa/Corbis, 84bl Michael DeYoung/Corbis, 85tl Franz Pfluegl/Dreamstime.com, 85br Jozsef Szasz-fabian/Dreamstime.com, 86-87 Visuals Unlimited/Corbis, 88cl Ioana Grecu/Dreamstime.com, 89bl Howard Sochurek/CORBIS, 92bl Rhonda Odonnell/Dreamstime.com, 92-93 Michael Rosenfeld/dpa/Corbis, 92tr Dreamstime. com, 93br Dario Sabljak/Dreamstime.com, 94tl Tim Pannell/Corbis, 94-95 Dreamstime.com, 95bl Galina Barskaya/Dreamstime.com, 96-97 Sebastian Kaulitzki/Dreamstime.com, 97tr Dreamstime.com, 97br Wa Li/Dreamstime.com, 98-99 Wa Li/Dreamstime.com, 100bl Eugene Bochkarev/Dreamstime.com, 101tc Visuals Unlimited/Corbis, 101br Dreamstime.com, 102-103 Dreamstime.com, 103cr Mediscan/Corbis, 103bc Heng kong Chen/Dreamstime.com, 105br Dreamstime.com, 106-107 Visuals Unlimited/Corbis, 108tr Jaimie Duplass/ Dreamstime.com, 108b Reuters/CORBIS, 109cl Matthew Mcvay/CORBIS, 110b Jeremy Horner/Corbis, 111tr Dreamstime.com, 111br Peggy Laflesh/Dreamstime.com, 112-113 Klaus Hackenberg/zefa/Corbis, 114r Dreamstime.com, 115cr Jason Stitt/Dreamstime.com, 115bc Gert Vrey/Dreamstime.com, 116r Olga Lyubkina/Dreamstime.com, 117tr Dreamstime.com, 117cr Ryan Pike/Dreamstime.com, 117bc Nicolas Nadjar/Dreamstime.com, 118l Linda Bucklin/Dreamstime.com, 118br Paul Moore/Dreamstime.com, 119br Dreamstime.com, 120-121 Don Mason/Corbis, 122-123 and 123tl Lester V. Bergman/CORBIS, 123tr Dreamstime.com, 123bl Howard Sochurek/CORBIS, 124-125 Micro Discovery/Corbis, 126-127 Dreamstime.com, 127t Howard Sochurek/CORBIS, 127br Dreamstime.com, 128-129 Visuals Unlimited/Corbis, 129cr Peter Jobst/Dreamstime.com, 130-131 Lester V. Bergman/ CORBIS, 131cr Tim Graham/Corbis, 133cr Tomasz Trojanowski/Dreamstime.com, 134-135 Dreamstime.com, 135tr Laurent Hamels/Dreamstime.com, 136-137 Holger Winkler/zefa/ Corbis, 136cl Dreamstime.com, 136bl Norma Cornes/Dreamstime.com, 137cr Dreamstime.com, 138-139 Lester V. Bergman/CORBIS, 141tr Ronnie Kaufman/CORBIS, 141cl verett Kennedy Brown/epa/Corbis, 141bc Dreamstime.com, 142 Bob Rowan; Progressive Image/CORBIS, 142cl Dreamstime.com, 143tr Roger Bruce/Dreamstime.com, 143bl Dreamstime.com, 144bl Kamil fazrin Rauf/Dreamstime.com, 145tl Yves Forestier/CORBIS SYGMA, 145cr Richard T. Nowitz/CORBIS, 147tl Doconnell/Dreamstime.com, 147tr Dreamstime.com, 147bl Loke Yek Mang/Dreamstime.com, 148-149 Asther Lau Choon Siew/Dreamstime.com, 149tl Alistair Scott/Dreamstime.com, 149bl Ilya Gridnev/Dreamstime.com, 150-151 Dreamstime.com, 151tl Lucian Coman/Dreamstime.com, 151bl Chris Townsend/Dreamstime.com, 152 Lorraine Swanson/Dreamstime.com, 153tr Roger Ressmeyer/CORBIS, 153bl all Dreamstime.com, 154 Ryszard Bednarek/Dreamstime.com, 155tr Alex Hinds/Dreamstime.com, 155br Owen Franken/Corbis, 156 Grafton Marshall Smith/CORBIS, 156bl Susan Tannenbaum/Dreamstime.com, 158-159 Jeff Lewis/Icon SMI/Corbis, 159tr Eddie Saab/Dreamstime.com, 160cr Dean Hoch/Dreamstime.com, 160b Gabe Palmer/CORBIS, 161tc Visuals Unlimited/Corbis, 161br Fred Goldstein/Dreamstime.com, 162tl Peter Dazeley/zefa/Corbis, 162bl Roger Ressmeyer/CORBIS, 162-163 John W. Gertz/zefa/Corbis, 163br Reuters/CORBIS, 164-165 Visuals Unlimited/Corbis, 166-167 Dreamstime.com, 167tr Dreamstime.com, 168br Gavin Wickham; Eye Ubiquitous/CORBIS, 169bl Eren Göksel/Dreamstime.com, 170bc Gordana Sermek/Dreamstime.com, 171t Dreamstime.com, 171bl Vladimir Pomortsev/Dreamstime.com, 172-173 and 173br Clouds Hill Imaging Ltd./Corbis, 174bl Daniel Gustavsson/Dreamstime.com, 175br Franz Pfluegl/Dreamstime.com, 176-177 Visuals Unlimited/Corbis, 177br Milan Kopcok/Dreamstime.com, 179tc Dreamstime.com, 179br Yanik Chauvin/Dreamstime.com, 180bl Reuters/CORBIS, 181tl Brett Mulcahy/Dreamstime.com, 181br Sandy Matzen/Dreamstime.com, 182b Dreamstime.com, 183tr Darrell Young/ Dreamstime.com, 183br Simone Van Den Berg/Dreamstime.com, 184bl Patrik Giardino/CORBIS, 185tr Natalie Fobes/CORBIS, 185br NASA, 186 Richard T. Nowitz/CORBIS, 187tl Dreamstime.com, 187br Louie Psihoyos/CORBIS, 188 Adrian Moisei/Dreamstime.com, 189br Jack Schiffer/Dreamstime.com, 189br Darius Ramazani/zefa/Corbis, 190-191 and 194bc RBM Online/Handout/Reuters/Corbis, 192l Manuel Moita/Dreamstime.com, 193br Sebastian Kaulitzki/Dreamstime.com, 194-195 Sebastian Kaulitzki/Dreamstime. com, 195tl Andres Rodriguez/Dreamstime.com, 195br Lester Lefkowitz/CORBIS, 196-197 Mediscan/Corbis, 196tr Jodi Baglien sparkes/Dreamstime.com, 196bc Natalia Sinjushina/ Dreamstime.com, 198 Jennie Woodcock; Reflections Photolibrary/CORBIS, 199tl Dreamstime.com, 199tr Dreamstime.com, 200-201 Rune Hellestad/Corbis, 201t Ingvald Kaldhussater/ Dreamstime.com, 201bl Dreamstime.com, 202tr Hanna Derecka/Dreamstime.com, 202b Jennie Woodcock; Reflections Photolibrary/CORBIS, 203t Zsolt Nyulaszi/Dreamstime.com, 203b Dreamstime.com, 204-205 Ryan Wasserman/Dreamstime.com, 205b Melissa King/Dreamstime.com, 206-207 Randy Faris/Corbis, 207cr LWA-Dann Tardif/CORBIS, 208-209 Jim Craigmyle/Corbis, 208tl Suzanne Tucker/Dreamstime.com, 208bl Marzanna Syncerz/Dreamstime.com, 209br Stanislav Tiplyashin/Dreamstime.com, 210-211 Mike Powell/ Corbis, 210br Dex Images/Corbis, 212-213 Glenda Powers/Dreamstime.com, 213bc Dreamstime.com, 215tc Howard Sochurek/CORBIS, 215br Dreamstime.com

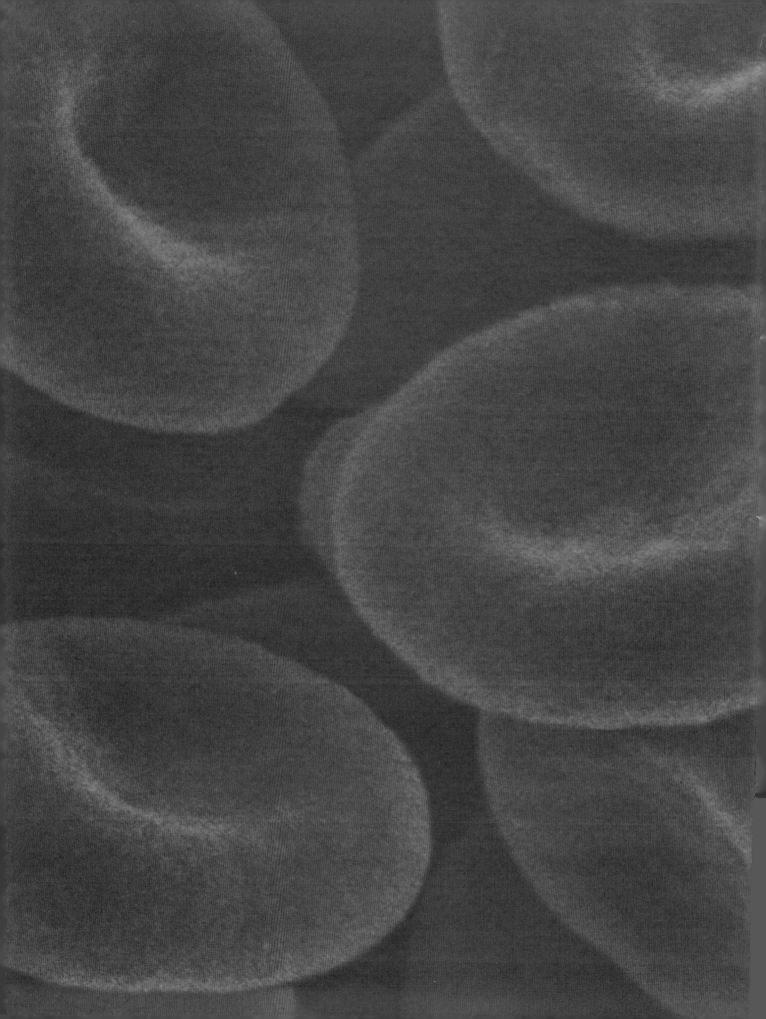